D0114385

Understanding Your Faith

A Christian Psychologist Helps You Look at Your Religious Experiences

H. Newton Malony

Understanding Your Faith

Understanding Your Faith

H. Newton Malony

Abingdon
Nashville

UNDERSTANDING YOUR FAITH

Copyright © 1978 by Abingdon

Library of Congress Cataloging in Publication Data

MALONY, H. NEWTON.
Understanding your faith.
Bibliography: p. 121
Includes index.
1. Faith. 2. Psychology, Religious. 3. Experience (Religion)
I. Title.
BV4637.M28   234'.3   78-8739

ISBN 0-675-42981-1

Scripture quotations unless otherwise noted are from the Revised
Standard Version of the Bible, copyrighted 1946, 1952, © 1971, 1973
by the Division of Christian Education of the National Council of the
Churches of Christ in the U.S.A. and are used by permission.

Scripture quotations noted Moffatt are from *The Bible: A New
Translation,* by James Moffatt; copyright 1935 by Harper & Row.

MANUFACTURED BY THE PARTHENON PRESS AT
NASHVILLE, TENNESSEE, UNITED STATES OF AMERICA

To Suzanna,
wife, companion, faithful pilgrim

Understanding Your Faith

Contents

Preface

Ours is a day of experience. Many persons have been born again. Numerous others report that they have met and talked with God. Religious experiences of many kinds are being sought out by a growing number of individuals. Indeed, most of us who will read this book can attest to times in our lives when we felt very close to the Divine.

What sense can we make of all this religious experiencing going on within us and all about us? How are we to understand the different experiences we have had across our lifetimes? Is there any way to comprehend the import and meaning of our faith that expresses itself in different ways and in varying degrees?

Most of us can report on our experiences from the inside. That is, we can recount the emotional feeling and the religious meaning of these events using the words of faith. But few of us have a broader understanding of these experiences. We feel uncertain of the psychological or environmental dimensions of what has happened to us. We are unable to tie together our religious experiences at different times in our lives in any satisfactory way.

This book is written to fill that need. It is offered in the spirit of Saint Augustine who defined theology as "faith seeking understanding." However, I write not about the content of faith, i.e. what one believes; I write about the experience of faith. In this sense, the book is called *Understanding Your Faith.* The emphasis is on the religious experience of the individual, not the Christian faith of the centuries.

I write as a Christian psychologist who has had numerous faith experiences across his lifetime. I make an effort to communicate some of the dynamics and determinants of such experiences from the viewpoint of modern psychology. Included are discussions on who has what experiences, why they have them, and what can be expected from them.

My hope is that the average religious person will profit from reading the volume. I think they will have a much broader appreciation of their own religious experience when they have finished. My intent is to enrich rather than diminish faith. I try to increase understanding without explaining faith away or reducing it to psychological dynamics. Hopefully, by reading this book, persons will become more committed at the same time that they become more knowledgeable.

My sincere thanks to Carol Burke whose patience and typing skill made this dream become a reality.

1. What Is Faith?

Faith is the assurance of things hoped for, the conviction of things not seen.—Hebrews 11:1

A friend said to me, "I go to church almost every Sunday. At some point in the service the pastor says, 'Let us affirm our faith together.' And we do it. We stand and read some words such as the Apostles Creed or a modern statement, etc. But I always feel a little confused. I ask myself—Is this my faith? What would I say if someone asked me to put faith in my own words? I rarely talk about my faith in between Sundays. Do I lose my faith when I don't say the words? Just what is faith?"

My friend is not alone in her confusion. She speaks for many of us who repeat statements of faith and live with our thoughts in between Sunday services. We, too, are perplexed about faith. We ask:

Where is faith? In our words? . . . In our thoughts? . . . In our deeds?

What is faith? Our feelings? . . . Our memories? . . . Our creeds?

When is faith? On Sunday morning? . . . Late at night? . . . While reciting Grace at mealtime?

The truth of the matter is: We have a lot of questions about faith. And they are far bigger than the mixture of feelings we have about affirming our faith on Sunday mornings.

Maybe we can reach a clearer understanding of faith if we put our minds to it. We have tended to put our religion off to the side of the rest of our lives. Perhaps it would help if we brought our faith into the middle of the arena. We could then look it square in the face and ask the same questions of it that we direct toward our politics, our preferences for certain recreations, and our friendships. In short, we could think reasonably about faith and use such disciplines as psychology to help us better understand this part of our lives.

For example, we could consider such questions as the following in light of what we know about the behavior of human beings (i.e. psychology):

1. What is faith?
2. Is faith more than words?
3. How does faith relate to religious experience?
4. Should we think of faith as a noun or a verb?
5. What does it mean to be a faithing person?

What Is Faith?

Many persons answer this question in terms of the *content* of faith. They will talk of the *Christian* faith, the

Buddhist faith, the *Unitarian* faith, or the *Muhammadan* faith. For them, faith is *what* people believe.

Persons with this viewpoint would say, "Your faith is in the words you say, the beliefs you hold." Thus, faith exists in the meaning of the creed. The statement of faith is faith.

Often, those with this view suggest that faith does not exist if the words are not correct. For example, they might say, "That creed is not Christian. That is not the Christian faith." Or they might say, "The Buddhist faith and the Muslim faith are not the same."

This definition puts an emphasis on the substance of faith—the words themselves—what is said. Faith is a noun. It is an entity. It exists outside persons. It is found in creeds.

An alternative to this position suggests that faith is a verb—not a noun. This means that faith is something persons do, not just a set of beliefs. It is a process, not an entity. If this is true, we can speak of persons *faithing* just as we speak of persons eating, running, or sleeping. Therefore, persons don't just *have* faith, they *do* faith. The entire eleventh chapter of the book of Hebrews supports this point of view.

The chapter begins by saying faith is the "assurance of things hoped for, the conviction of things not seen" (v. 1). Faith equals assurance plus conviction. Note how many of the verses begin:

Through faith we understand . . . v. 3 (KJV)
By faith Abel offered unto God . . . v. 4
By faith Enoch was translated . . . v. 5
By faith Noah . . . prepared . . . v. 7

By faith Abraham . . . obeyed . . . v. 8
Through faith Sara . . . received strength . . . v. 11
These all died in faith . . . v. 13
By faith Isaac blessed Jacob . . . v. 20
By faith Moses, . . . was hid three months . . . v. 23
Through faith he kept the passover . . . v. 28
By faith they passed through the Red sea . . . v. 29

A powerful statement can be found in verses 32-33. "And what more shall I say? For time would fail me to tell of Gideon, Barak, Samson, Jephthah, of David and Samuel and the prophets— who through faith conquered kingdoms, enforced justice, received promises, stopped the mouths of lions."

By, through, in—these are all process words. They speak of faith as a means to an end. Being assured of things hoped for and being convicted of things not seen becomes the means by which persons understand, prepare, obey, pass through, conquer, die, etc. Faith undergirds or lies beneath these acts. This is what it means to live by faith or to live faithingly. Thus, it is not so much the beliefs as the act of believing.

Is Faith More Than Words?

If we accept that faith is something more than a set of beliefs, then we would have to answer yes. As has been said, faith is a human process whereby persons obtain the courage to live religiously. Scripture speaks of persons who *"live* by faith" (Galatians 2:20).

We see the "living" and assume that faith lies underneath. It is like the foundation of a house, the pipe through which water flows. The paper on which words are printed, the air in which the airplane rides, or the track on which the runner runs.

A diagram of this understanding of faith as the unseen, but very active and dynamic, process underlying life is given below:

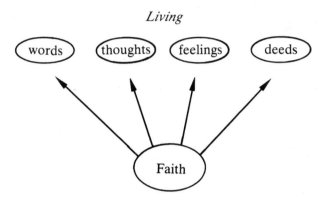

Living

words   thoughts   feelings   deeds

Faith

Note that the lines shoot up from *faith* to *living.* Faith influences the words, thoughts, feelings and deeds of living. Faith as the deep "assurance of things hoped for" and the inner "conviction of things not seen" permeates the words we say, the thoughts in our minds, the feelings we have, and the acts we undertake.

We Never See Faith

Think about it for a moment. You never see faith. What you do see is people expressing their feelings, reporting their thoughts, speaking their convictions and intentions, and engaging in action. Those are the only events we observe. That is what it means to live—to think, feel, speak, and act. Faith is the convictions and assurances—yes, the fermenting, effervesence process that erupts through and guides these behaviors.

We never see faith. But we infer that it's there. Have we not all heard, "Jim has a strong faith" or "Elizabeth's faith is wavering" or "Mac has lost his faith" or "Mary, where is your faith"? All these statements are inferences we make from seeing or hearing behavior, (i.e. thoughts, words, feelings, actions).

Faith as Attitude and Perception

Turning to a different issue, What do we find when we go beneath behavior and look more closely at the inner process we call faith? Another way of asking it is, If we look faith in the face, what do we see?

Hebrews 11:1 gives us a hint in saying that faith is an assurance and a conviction.

On the one hand, assurances and convictions are what psychologists call "attitudes." On the other hand, they are what psychologists call "perceptions."

Attitudes are like attention getters. When we say that a person has a good attitude, we mean that that person is inclined to respond positively. For example, having a good attitude toward football probably implies that a person will look at football games on TV if given a chance to choose between that and a soap opera. A bad attitude implies a rejection of something. Faith is having a positive attitude toward God and hoping for a future in which he will have a part. God has caught that person's attention.

Perceptions are like insights. They imply that one knows the truth. When we say, "I perceive how it is," we imply that we know the real truth. It is like saying, "I understand." Perceptions always go beyond the facts or the obvious. They stretch the truth, so to speak. For example, when a person says, "I perceive or understand the truth about the major," they are adding their interpretation to the evidence, and it is convincing to them. Faith is the perception of the truth about God and life. It is a conviction about things "not seen."

Faith Is Response

Bringing together these ideas about assurances, convictions, attitudes, and perceptions, we could say that faith is a *response.*

Faith is not simply a reaction. That is, it is more than just shutting one's eyes when a bright light is turned on or pulling one's hand away from a hot stove. Faith is not a reflex action, done without any thought. Some human behavior is like that—knee jerks, cuddling in a mother's arms, being startled when the elevator moves swiftly. But faith is much more than this.

Faith is a response. The person does something with the information he or she gets before reacting. Thought and reflection go on inside the person in a response. Below is a diagram of the way this distinction between reacting and responding is sometimes understood.

$$S \longrightarrow R \quad = \quad \text{a reaction}$$
$$S \longrightarrow O \longrightarrow R \quad = \quad \text{a response}$$

S stands for the stimulus or situation, *O* stands for the organism (or person) and *R* stands for the reaction or the response. In a *reaction* nothing goes on inside the person. It is like a reflex which takes no thought. In a *response* the person thinks about what is happening before responding.

Faith is much more a response than a reaction. There is nothing automatic or instinctive about faith. It is not a reflex. Faith is well considered. The assurances, attitudes, convictions, and perceptions which make up faith go on inside the person. They are the processes that occur before a response is made.

Faith: A Response to What?

Faith always has an object outside itself to which it responds. Faith is not faith in oneself but faith in a being one calls God. And God is outside the person.

Recall that in the discussion of faith as response, a stimulus came before the response. This stimulus is God. A diagram of faith would, therefore, look like this:

God (stimulus) ⟶ O (person) ⟶ Faith (response)

From a Christian point of view, this makes good sense. Christian faith could be defined as response to the God who has come to mankind in Jesus Christ. As Hebrews 1:1-2 states, "In many and various ways God spoke of old to our fathers by the prophets; but in these last days he has spoken to us by a Son, whom he appointed the heir of all things, through whom also he created the world."

Christian faith is a response to the God who has acted in Christ. Faith is the assurance of things hoped for—namely, our longing for a Savior. Faith is also the conviction of things not seen—namely, the belief that God is with us even though we have never seen him. Faith is a response to the revelation of God in Christ as it comes to us through Scripture, the proclamation of the church, and the witness of other persons.

Faith is the totally human response to this totally divine event—God in Christ.

Our emphasis in this chapter has been on the faith response instead of the revelation object of that faith. Yet it goes without saying that faith, to be faith, must have an object to respond to. And the object of Christian faith is God, the father of our Lord Jesus Christ.

How Does Religious Experience Relate to Faith?

When we have a religious experience, is that the same thing as having faith? For example, if I am moved by the worship service and tears come to my eyes, is this faith? The answer is yes and no.

Religious experience is a term that could be applied to the whole revelation/faith/response event. Faith is a part of that but not all of it. It could be diagramed this way:

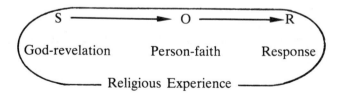

Very often people talk about religious experience as if it applied to only a part of this. They will say, "Suddenly,

I heard a voice call my name, and no one was there. It must have been God." Or they will say, "I was looking for an answer to prayer when I found this verse in the Bible." The danger is that they think of religious experience as a strange event in which God appears to them. But religious experience includes the process of faith and the subsequent response, also. It involves inner-reflection leading to assurance and conviction (faith) out of which comes trustful behavior (the response). Taken together they comprise religious experience.

Summing up this chapter, the following could be said:

1. Many of us wonder what faith is.
2. Faith is more the act of believing than a set of beliefs.
3. Faith lies underneath behavior.
4. Faith is a process containing assurance and conviction.
5. Faith is a response, not a reaction.
6. Christian faith is a response to God in Christ.
7. Religious experience includes the whole revelation—faith—response event.

With these thoughts in mind, let us turn in the next chapter to a consideration of the different expressions of faith.

2. What Causes Faith to Occur?

They said to each other, "Did not our hearts burn within us while he talked to us on the road, while he opened to us the scriptures"—(Luke 24:32)?"

Faith occurs at some pretty odd places and times. On the dusty road to Emmaus, indeed. Yet this is no less strange than some of my friends who report:

"It happened to me as I was driving to work. . . . "
"I felt my body covered with goosepimples, and my mind was awestruck at the grandeur of that sunrise. . . . "
"I had drunk several beers when my roommate's Bible caught my eye. I began to read . . . and then . . . ."

"When I was kneeling at the church altar, I could not hold back the tears . . . of joy . . . of thanks. . . . "

"We talked way into the night as the campfire burned low. Later that night in my tent . . . ."

"It suddenly became clear to me after long hours of study . . . ."

"I was overwhelmed by the beauty of the altar and the colors of the windows . . . ."

Faith is a puzzle. It sometimes feels like an unpredictable contagion that strikes first here and then there. Where it will land, nobody knows. It sometimes happens here. It doesn't happen there. When we seek it, it is elusive. When we least expect it, it often comes. It is frequently weak. It is sometimes strong. Gather people together, some will have the experience, others will not. At other times, when persons are apart, they report a similar occurrence.

So we are faced with such facts as these:

same person—different experiences
same experience—different persons
different times—same experience
similar times—different experiences
same experience—different places
same place—different experiences

The puzzle is this: Why does faith happen in the first place? When is faith most likely to occur? Who has faith experiences, and who does not? Where can faith be predicted to happen? Psychology can help us to answer these questions.

Why Faith?

When we ask "why", we are looking for the reason something happens. For example, "Why does the grass grow?" means "What causes it to sprout and spread out and grow tall?" We feel we have given good reasons when we answer, "The grass grows because it is watered and because it is planted in soil that is rich with nitrogen."

So "why" means "causes," "reasons," and "things that make other things happen." This is often spoken of as looking for a cause-effect relationship. A diagram of this relationship would look something like this:

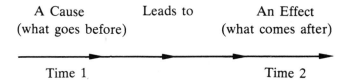

A Cause	Leads to	An Effect
(what goes before)		(what comes after)
Time 1		Time 2

A cause always occurs before, or leads up to, an effect. When we look for causes (or ask why), we usually are thinking back and trying to explain the reason something has happened. And we usually assume that everything has a cause, do we not?

So it is with faith. We see somebody that has faith, and we wonder what caused it, led up to it, explained it. We see faith in somebody, and we say "They have faith because. . . ." We assume it did not occur by chance. It had to have a cause.

A Cause for Faith?

Some persons will think it awkward to consider faith this way. They prefer to think of faith as something that happened or happens to them out of the blue—without any reason to cause it. They report experiences in which God or faith was the farthest thing from their minds. They insist they did not plan for it, nor did they seek it. It just happened. The famous psychologist William James supported this point of view when he said that faith came from the unconscious mind. By this, he meant that the persons he studied had little or no idea from whence their experience came, i.e. what caused it.

Other persons insist that God causes faith and that any effort to find human reasons for it will be fruitless. Dialogue has continued about this among religious scholars. In this century, Karl Barth represented those who felt that faith occurs because God awakens people's minds and hearts to the truth of the gospel. Faith, to Barth and others, does not have any earthly causes. We look in vain for such reasons for faith, they suggest.

Even John Wesley, who put much emphasis on the individual search for God, had a doctrine he called prevenient grace whereby God gave persons the interest in and the power to seek faith. According to Wesley, faith was not man-made but God-given.

An anonymous hymn illustrates this opinion:

> I sought the Lord, and afterward I knew
>   He moved my soul to seek him, seeking me;
> It was not I that found, O Savior true;

No, I was found of thee.
Thou didst reach forth thy hand and mine enfold;
   I walked and sank not on the storm-vexed sea;
'Twas not so much that I on thee took hold
   As thou, dear Lord, on me.

I find, I walk, I love, but oh, the whole
   Of love is but my answer, Lord, to thee!
For thou wert long beforehand with my soul;
   Always thou lovedst me.

Causes: Human and Divine

There is a way, however, to think about *causes* without denying the place of God in the experience of faith. We can certainly affirm that God reaches out to us in the sending of Jesus to live, die, and rise from the dead here on this earth. The story of that love comes to us through the Bible. It is the reality which lies behind our faith. God is the stimulus to which we respond in faith. This is what was suggested in chapter 1 when faith was diagramed in this manner:

God (stimulus) ⟶ O (person) ⟶ Faith (response)

Thus, in this sense, God causes faith.

Further, we can affirm that whenever a person responds in faith to God (the stimulus), they do so because God has created them capable of responding to him. This is to say that God made persons in such a way that they have a need for him. As Saint Augustine said in his memorable prayer, "Thou has made us for Thyself, and our hearts are restless till they find their rest in Thee." This restlessness inside us is like Wesley's prevenient grace. It is a God-given restlessness, a built-in need for God. So faith occurs because God has made it possible. We could rediagram the relationship below to include this dimension:

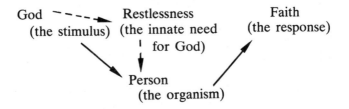

Thus, God causes faith. He is the stimulus to which persons respond, and he created persons to need him. However, if this were all there is to it, everyone would have faith. And this is not true. The beginning of this chapter illustrated the fact that faith sometimes occurs, and sometimes it does not. It happens in some places but not in others, at some times and not others, and in some people and not others. To make sense out of this puzzle, we need to add human to the divine causes noted above.

In other words, God (either as stimulus or creator) does not overwhelm our humanness. The way we respond is filtered through our personality, our predicaments, our situations, and our minds. At a given point, whether we respond in faith or not is determined by things inside us just as much as by God. In this sense, there are human causes for faith—i.e., human events that lead up to or help explain faith.

Causes: Necessary and Sufficient

One way of thinking about this is to say *God* is the "necessary" cause while *we* are the "sufficient" cause of faith. The distinction between necessary and sufficient causes has been talked about for a long time. Necessary causes are those things that must be present for an event to occur. Without these basic conditions things will not happen. They are the foundations. For example, a plant will not grow without soil. Neither will a book be printed without paper. Moreover, an airplane will not fly without wings. These are necessary causes. But by themselves, they will not cause an event. It takes something else. These are the sufficient causes.

Sufficient causes are those that make a thing happen once the necessary causes are present. For example, water will make a plant grow if it is in good soil. Typeset that is inked will result in printing if there is enough paper in the press. Wind will make an airplane fly if it is built with adequate wing span. Water, inked typeset, and wind are sufficient causes. They trigger an event if the basics are present.

God is the necessary and man is the sufficient cause for faith. Faith will occur when persons are ripe and ready, if God has created a need for himself in people and if he has presented himself to them through Jesus Christ. Now we affirm that God has made himself known to us in Jesus Christ and that he has created human beings to have a need for him. What we don't know are the human conditions that seem to trigger faith or impede it.

Some of the reasons why we respond in faith at one time but not at another are understood to us. Much of the time they are far less clear. It is easy to empathize with those who seem to not ever know where their faith comes from. We spoke earlier of those who report their faith as coming out of the blue, that is as being unexplainable. The rest of this chapter is addressed to describing these human causes that underlie and help explain our faith.

Needs and Interests Equal Motives

All human behavior, including faith, is caused by needs, according to psychologists. Need is the term which refers to those basic impulses inside each and every person. They are the things that a person has to have in order to live. They are the urges that get people moving and sustain them in their endeavors. Needs are thought of as foundations, as basics, as generalities, as universals.

Interests, on the other hand, are specific wants. They direct behavior after needs get the action started. They are the desires we have for definite persons, activities, or objects in our surroundings which will satisfy the basic needs we have.

A familiar illustration has to do with eating. I say, "I'm hungry." Hunger is a need. It is a general feeling. The need does not say what I am hungry for or direct me to what I will eat. Interests do that. So, I continue, "I think I'll cook myself a hamburger." The desire for a hamburger is an interest. It is a specific food available to me which will satisfy my hunger need.

Needs plus interests equal motives. Motives are the causes for our action, the reason we behave as we do. When faith occurs, we can safely say, therefore, that there was present inside the person a need for God and an interest in the particular religious activity available at the moment. An illustration would be a person who has a faith experience while hearing a sermon at church. This implies a need for God, which is the underlying cause for making a person attentive and aware. It further implies an interest in sermons per se, which is a particular way of meeting one's need for God. Just as one can meet his or her need for food in a variety of ways so one can meet his or her need for God in various manners.

One further comment about needs and interest: One interest can meet several needs, and one need can be met through several interests. For example, eating hamburgers can meet a need for hunger and a need to be with other people. Further, a hunger need can be met through several interests, e.g., an interest in Italian food, an interest in Kentucky Fried Chicken, and an interest in potluck dinners at the church. So it is with faith. A given faith interest, e.g., in revival meetings, can meet the need for God and the need for fun and the need for fellowship. Moreover, a need for God can be met through interests in Bible reading, attendance at a course on C. S. Lewis, meditation alone in an empty church, or arising to see the sunrise.

Few Needs, Many Interests

There are only a few needs, but there are many interests. Interests vary from culture to culture, but needs are the same wherever people are found.

The needs of persons could be subsumed under four headings: *survival, satisfaction, security,* and *self-discovery.* I feel these four *Ss* lie beneath all the varied interests in which we see persons involved, including faith.

The *survival* need is the drive to stay alive and to maintain one's existence. We can see this need expressed in such interests as buying warm winter clothes, jogging to increase one's blood circulation, planning a budget that will assure nutritious meals, and accepting Christ as the Savior whose Father will bring one back to life at the time of the final judgment.

The *satisfaction* need is the drive to find pleasure and enjoyment in the events of life. It is the old tendency to seek pleasure and avoid pain. We can see this need expressed in such interests as going to a party, sweetening one's coffee, taking a cruise on a ship, joining in a chuch youth rally, watching TV, collecting stamps, or singing hymns.

The *security* need is the drive to find a place, surety, safety, and predictability in life. This can be seen in an interest in finding one's vocation, obeying one's parents, deciding who one will marry, reading theology, joining a club, being a good citizen, studying the history of one's country, attending a training school for a trade, and reading the newspaper.

The *self-discovery* need is the drive to find identity, meaning, purpose, and fulfillment for oneself. We can see this expressed all the way from reading the Bible to going to an encounter group, to looking for a new job, to talking with friends way into the night, to reading literature, to praying and meditating, to listening to lectures by wise persons.

Now faith would seem to be related most to the needs

for security and for self-discovery. When we have faith experiences it can be assumed that we are meeting, to some degree, our needs for knowing who we are, for finding a secure role for ourselves in life, for deciding on the purpose for our life, and for settling the question of whether life has any meaning or not.

However, let it not be simply assumed that whenever persons engage in an event in which they experience God that they are only meeting their needs for security and self-discovery. My wife is an example. She sings in our choir at church and often is deeply moved by the experience. To be sure the singing is an affirmation of her faith, but it is also a very pleasureful event for her. In this sense, it meets her satisfaction needs. She would just as soon sing on Thursday nights as to watch TV.

Suffice it to say that the human cause through which faith is filtered is this set of human needs. Particularly, faith becomes paramount when persons feel a need for security and self-discovery. When persons experience these needs, they are peculiarly susceptible to faith experiences. When they do not feel these needs, they will be less likely to experience God.

Basic Anxieties

Five components of the security and self-discovery needs are worthy of discussion. They are the typical ways in which persons recognize that these underlying needs are active in them. They are the fairly normal anxieties which lead to faith. These are anxieties of time, identity, place, causality, and substance. They have been called the basic anxieties.

First, there is the anxiety of *time* which is an indication of the need for security. This is the awareness of the passage of the years and the inability one has to make time stand still. One sees alteration and deterioration. One cannot stop memory from being both exhilarating and frightening at the same time. In the midst of all this change and unalterable movement of the clock, there is anxiety coupled with a desire to find something on which to hold that is not ravaged by time. Faith in God is an experience of the timeless.

Next, there is the anxiety of *identity,* which is an indication of the need for self-discovery. This is the awareness that a person wants a role to play in life that will be accepted and approved by others. Further, it has to be a role one feels is right for him or her. The market keeps changing in its demands. People are fickle. They approve at one time and reject at another. In the midst of this search for meaning, there is anxiety resulting from the desire to find an identity for oneself that will last and will not change. Faith in God is an experience of finding permanent identity.

Third, there is the anxiety of *place,* which is an indication of the need for security. This is the awareness that the ground underneath one is unstable. It is constantly shifting, and it can be sold out from underneath if monthly payments are not made. The changing economy makes money values change and the price of providing a place for oneself remarkedly fluid. In the midst of this search, there is anxiety coupled with a compulsion to carve out for oneself a home to call one's own. Faith in God is an experience of finding firm ground on which to stand.

Then, there is the anxiety of *causality* which is an indication of the need for self-discovery. This is the awareness of one's powerlessness and of one's fragility. There is a sense of not having determined to be where one finds oneself and of having little power to dictate one's future. In the midst of this desire for strength and self-determination, there is anxiety coupled with a drive to have a part in one's destiny. Faith in God is an experience of One who has all things in his hands.

Finally, there is the anxiety of *substance,* which is an indication of the need for self-discovery. This is the sense that one is made of nothing that lasts. There is the awareness of one's body as made up of organs that wear out over time and of one's strength as ebbing and flowing from time to time. In the midst of this feeling of frailness, there is anxiety coupled with a strong desire to be made of sterner stuff, to affirm a part of oneself that will outlast the deterioration. Faith in God is an experience of One who assures us of eternal life.

These are the felt anxieties which tell us our needs are aroused. How these anxieties will be alleviated depends on the variety of faith experiences available to us. The variety is endless, but the needs and anxieties are the same from person to person. As has been said by the theologian Paul Tillich, "Life poses the questions to which faith is the answer."

Causes: Known and Unknown

Earlier in this chapter, it was said that many people do not acknowledge any needs or anxieties which precede their faith experiences. However, we have said that where there is no need or anxiety or interest, there will be no faith. How can these two observations be reconciled?

A helpful model for understanding this suggests that there is a period of preparation, a moment of decision, after which there is a period of follow up to faith. The period of preparation may last for a short or a long time. It may be more conscious at some time than at others. When persons say that they are not aware of any need or anxiety just before their faith experience, it is probably due to the fact that the period of preparation for them has lasted a long time. The anxieties to which faith comes as answers have, most likely, been long-lasting. They have become subconscious but are still powerful. At the moment of decision or faith the person may not be aware of them. But they are still there. Often during the follow up period, a person will respond to the faith event in a way that makes it clear that faith was an answer to deep anxieties. So let it be said that the needs are always present whether one is conscious of them or not.

In summary, this chapter has suggested that:

1. Faith occurs in some places and at some times but not always.
2. This leads to the question Why?
3. To ask why is to ask for the causes or reasons for something.
4. There are two causes for faith—human and divine.
5. God causes faith by being the stimulus to which

we respond, that is, he comes to us in Jesus Christ, and by creating us with a need for him.

6. God is the necessary cause, but we human beings are the sufficient causes for faith, that is, our needs dictate whether we experience faith or not.
7. Human needs are general urges. Human interests are specific attractions. Needs provoke behavior. Interests direct behavior.
8. There are four basic human needs: survival, security, satisfaction, and self-discovery.
9. Five basic anxieties indicate our need for God: They are the anxieties over time, identity, place, causality, substance.
10. All faith experiences are based on needs whether persons are conscious of these needs or not.

3. Kinds of Faith

When I was a child, I spoke like a child, I thought like a child. . . . But now that I am a man I have given up childish ways. Once I saw through a glass darkly, but now I see face to face, and know, even as I am known.—1 Corinthians 13:11

In the first chapter faith was defined. In the second chapter faith was explained. In this chapter, the different kinds of faith will be described.

Faith, as it was defined, is an inner response of belief and trust in God. It is a perception of how things really are. It is an insight into the meaning of life. It is an attitude that makes persons ready to act in trusting, loving, faithful ways.

Faith, as it was explained, occurs in response to person's needs for survival, satisfaction, security, and self-discovery. While faith can meet all those needs or any combination of them, it usually is an answer to the search for self-discovery. It meets person's basic anxieties over the passage of time, the elusiveness of status, the desire for power, and the frailty of the physical body. Underneath faith, there is cause-effect relationship with these basic anxieties even though we do not always recognize it.

Thus, whenever, wherever, and to whomever faith occurs, it is basically the same as its core. Underneath the surface, from the inside out, all faith is alike. The faith of a teen-ager from Iowa, a mountaineer from Kentucky, a nurse from Louisiana, a child from New York City, or a retired teacher in Florida is all alike. At its essence, each of these faiths is a personal response to God which answers one of life's basic anxieties. Whether they look alike or not, whether they use the same words to describe it or admit it, the truth is that they are the same!

Yet, in another respect, there are obvious differences. On the surface, from the outside, all faith is not the same. Faith comes in different kinds (or flavors). It occurs at different places and times. And last, but not least important, it happens inside different people. While these differences are alike at their core, i.e., in terms of their dynamics, they are, nevertheless, important and worthy of our attention. Therefore, let us turn to a description of these various kinds of faith, acknowledging, as we do, that to the naked eye, faith certainly appears as if it is not the same from time to time or person to person.

Abraham: A Good Example

Abraham is a good example of how faith changes from time to time in a person's life. The book of Genesis recounts at least five faith experiences in the life of Abraham. They were:

1. his call to be the father of many nations (12:1-5)
2. his division of the land with Lot (13:1-15)
3. his being visited by angels who announce the birth of Isaac (18:1-17)
4. his near sacrifice of Isaac (22:1-14)
5. his seeking of a bride for Isaac (24:1-67)

Each of these occurred at different times in his life. Although it was definitely the same God with whom he was interacting, these events do not, on the surface, appear to be answers to the same problems and, most certainly, were not simple replications of each other.

Abraham's initial call to be "the father of many nations" appears to come from out of the blue. He did not seem to be seeking fame or fortune. Much less did he want to leave his homeland, pick up stakes, and move out to a "land he knew not where." Yet, God spoke to him and he chose to respond to faith, by trusting God to lead him. The experience ended with his moving out on faith to follow where God might lead him. This happened in the land of Ur at the time of early civilization.

Remember Abraham's initial faith experience? It pertained to a promise of a new land that God promised to Abraham. Land had great religious meaning to persons in that day. So it is not surprising that when trouble broke out between the herdsmen of Abraham and his brother Lot that Abraham should seek a faith answer to the problem. The division of the land between the two of them was, for Abraham, under the direction of God. He prayed about it and asked God's direction. His response to the problem was based on faith.

Later on, when Abraham was much older, he was living on the desert with his wife, Sarah. We get the feeling that life had been somewhat disappointing to him because he and Sarah had borne no children. One day, angels came to visit him. They told him that Sarah, who was aged by this time, would conceive and bear a child. One of the humorous incidents of the Bible is the picture of Sarah giggling out loud in another part of the tent when she heard the visitors predict that she would bear a child. Yet Abraham and Sarah trusted God; they had faith.

Some time after this, Isaac was born and, like many other children, became a precious person in the eyes of his father. One day, when Isaac was still a child, Abraham had another faith experience. He felt God was telling him to take Isaac out and demonstrate his love for God by killing Isaac as a sacrifice. Abraham was greatly troubled but proceeded to do as God commanded. Just before Abraham killed Isaac, God spoke a word of reassurance and told Abraham to sacrifice a sheep instead. This certainly appears to be a different type of faith experience than Abraham had ever had before!

Finally, the seeking of a bride for Isaac was a faith experience. The scripture reads: "Abraham was old and well stricken with age: and the Lord had blessed

Abraham in all things" (Genesis 24:1). At this time, toward the end of his life, Abraham sent his servants to his homeland to find a bride for Isaac—as he felt God would have him do. The familiar story of Rebecca at the well confirmed Abraham's faith. Soon thereafter, Abraham died peacefully.

It is easy to see when we look at Abraham that faith looks and feels different from time to time in a person's life. Years of experience bring different problems and outlooks. We might hypothesize that Abraham was more optimistic and hopeful early in his life than at the time when he and Sarah were bemoaning their lack of a child. The times of conflict over the sacrifice of Isaac and the dispersal of grazing lands were unlike the early period of great anticipation or the peaceful calm of the later years in Canaan, when the land had been found and Isaac had been married to Rebecca. And death brings its own anxieties that cannot be anticipated earlier in life.

There is, thus, the faith of childhood, of young man/womanhood, of adulthood, and of death. Many of us, like Abraham, can remember encounters with God at several points in life. Change has occurred. The issues feel different. Faith differs from time to time.

Personal Development and Change

Ideally, faith develops and deepens as time goes on. This means that the faith of adulthood ought to cover more ground, meet more needs, include more dimensions, be more real than the faith of childhood. Abraham's faith seemed to be so. Although circumstances changed, his faith experiences broadened, expanded, and matured. A diagram of Abraham's faith might look like the one below. The ascending line represents his deepening and developing faith over the passing years and under different circumstances.

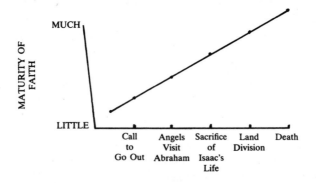

However, life does not always live up to the ideal. Faith does not always grow deeper and more mature. It often fluctuates from time to time in such a fashion that later faith experience may be less well developed than it was at an earlier time. John Wesley wrote much about the tendency to "fall from grace." We have all experienced faith that is strong at one time and weak at another. This seems to be far more typical than Abraham's example of continued growth.

Peter's faith is an illustration of this up and down change that many of us have experienced in our faith experiences. The Bible recounts at least seven events in Peter's story. They were:

1. his call to cease fishing and follow Jesus (Matt. 4:18-30);
2. his attempt to walk on the water (Matt. 14:22-32);

3. his confession that Jesus was the Christ at Caesarea Phillipi (Matt. 16:13-20);
4. his denial at the time of Jesus' crucifixion (Matt. 26:69-75);
5. his recognition of the resurrected Lord after he had gone back to fishing (John 21:1-14);
6. his healing in the Temple as he preached the gospel (Acts 3:1-11); and
7. his going to Joppa to preach to the Gentiles after having a vision from God (Acts 10:23-48).

These familiar stories illustrate a definite fluctuation in the depth and assurance Peter felt in his faith experience. There were times of doubt and of confusion as well as moments of great conviction and security. Peter's faith could be diagramed as follows. Again, the up-and-down line represents the depth and maturity of his faith over the passing years and under different circumstances.

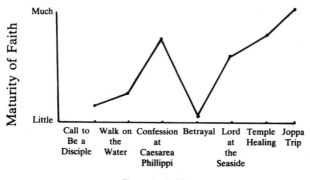

Peter's Life

For Peter, faith experiences ebbed and flowed. They came and went in terms of their power and their effect. As for many of us, God was more real to him at some times than at others.

Now, let us turn away from a discussion of changes in faith over time within the same person to a consideration of differences in faith experiences between people.

Another Example: Two High School Boys

Differences, from time to time for the same person are not as dramatic as those between persons at a given point in life. The experience of my son and a friend of his illustrate these distinctions.

Bill was my son's friend. We saw him at school on parent's night in mid-fall of their last year of junior high school. "Do you see that boy, Dad?" my son asked me. "Sure," I replied. "Well, he got saved this summer. He's really changed. He doesn't curse and tell dirty jokes anymore. He reads Scripture and prays daily. I've never had that happen to me. I sure hope it does sometime." Well, it didn't—at least not at that time.

Some four years later, Michael, my son, graduated from high school. At breakfast one day in the middle of summer, he asked me this question: "Dad, can I wear this necklace of yours?" I noticed he had on a pendant shaped like a fish which had been given to me on my birthday. "Of course," I replied. "Do you know what the fish symbol means?" "Yes indeed," he answered. "It means I am a Christian. My faith is coming to mean much more to me these days, and I want to keep it on all the time." In a quiet and nondramatic way he was having a faith experience similar to but distinctly unlike his friend Bill's of some four years before.

A few weeks later, my son went off to college. I received a telephone call from him late on Sunday evening. "Dad," he said, "I thought you'd like to know, I just accepted the Lord." Here was the experience he had been looking for. It came after hearing of his girl friend's rededication of herself at a weekend retreat and a period of prayer with his buddies in the dorm room.

Bill's experience had occurred at the close of a revival service at his church when he was fourteen years old. Michael's had occurred in the privacy of his own bedroom and was provoked by seeing a necklace on my dresser when he was eighteen. Differences between persons are marked and important.

The variety is almost endless. Any of you who have ever been to a testimony meeting or a sharing group will agree. Faith experiences come in all shapes and sizes. In another volume, *Ways People Meet God,* I have recounted experiences in the lives of a group of persons I know.

First, there was Don who came alive to faith by secretly reading the Bible in a cubbyhole of a university library. Next, there was Lynn who suddenly found herself praying in a new language as she knelt at the altar during a prayer service. Then there was Lee who became excited, tingly, and enthused at a worship service after an absence of forty years from the church. Further, there was Dan who begrudgingly went to evangelism training and found himself immensely excited when the first person he contacted accepted Christ. Next, there was Phyllis who eagerly read a book by Paul Tillich way into the night after attending a class at her church. Then there was Barbie who joined a Christian commune and found enough support to give up drugs. Finally, there was Al who heard a sermon which provoked him to repent of his vulgarity and worldliness and become a staunch church member.

The list could go on. Even in the Bible we see differences ranging from the quiet faith of Timothy to the radical conversion of Paul; from the nighttime call of Samuel to the insight of Jonah in the midst of storm; from the loyal adoration of Mary, the mother, to the forgiven restoration of Mary, the Magdelene; and from the rational confrontation of Nicodemus to the awestruck belief of a Corinthian jailer.

Faith experiences are filtered through our unique circumstances. The time and the place is always different for each of us even though we may be together at a given moment. Each of us looks at life through our own eyes. We stand in our own shoes and live out of our own understandings. So it would not be surprising that faith is expressed in unique and personal ways again and again.

Kinds of Faith: A Model

A descriptive list of all the different types of faith experiences people have would be interesting. It would be more helpful, however, if we had a model into which we could place all of these events which would allow us to understand them more fully. Thus, we would be able to talk about a given situation as if it illustrated a certain kind of faith experience. For example, take the case of Phyllis, noted earlier. She came to a new understanding of herself as a child of God by reading a book by Paul

Tillich shortly after attending a class at her church. A model might describe this as an intellectual faith experience in a middle-aged woman. Further, it might be described as the first such religious event in her life since childhood. Finally, it was moderate in intensity and lasted for several months.

The model, as may be apparent, includes the dimensions of:

1. the age at which the faith occurs;
2. the type of emphasis in the experience (i.e., emotional or intellectual),
3. the locale of the experience (i.e., whether it occurred alone or with other persons);
4. the frequency of the experiences in the life of the individual;
5. the depth, importance or intensity of the experience;
6. the duration or length of the event.

Another example will illustrate the utility of such an approach. Consider Abraham's division of the land with Lot. The model would describe this as intellectual experience of moderate intensity and short duration in an aging person. We have the impression that by this time in Abraham's life he was constantly turning things over to God for his direction. Thus the experience happened frequently. Also, Abraham was an old man whose faith was deep and profound. It was an intellectual decision based on the conviction that God had a plan and purpose for every event. It was very important to Abraham to have Lot's goodwill and to be led by God. However, the experience was short-lived in that Abraham made the decision and turned his mind to other matters.

That faith experiences differ from each other in these dimensions should be quite clear by now. Obviously, persons begin to have faith experiences early in childhood and continue to have them until the time of their deaths. Thus, age, at the time of the experience, is important. Again, experiences seem to be of two dominant types that occur in isolation or combination. Persons report feelings of emotion ranging all the way from awe to guilt to release to acceptance. They also report insights and understandings ranging from leaps of faith to resolutions to problems of meaning. Thus, an emotional-intellectual distinction in type of faith experience. These emphases are often combined, of course.

Further, faith experiences occur in different locales. Locale can mean place or person. Faith can occur at church, at work, at play, at school, at war, or at camp, to name a few of the many places. Faith can also occur alone, with a few others, in a crowd, or where two or more are gathered in worship. In fact, faith experiences can and have occurred at any conceivable place in the presence or absence of any group of people.

Moreover, frequency is a strategic dimension. How often faith experiences have happened before is a helpful thing to know. Many persons attend charismatic prayer meetings regularly expecting a certain faith experience to occur time after time. At the other extreme, there is the once-in-a-lifetime experience of answering the preacher's invitation to give your life to fulltime Christian service. This is a memory I have from my sixteenth year. It still stands out as a singular, one-time- only event that has never repeated.

Intensity has two aspects. Faith experience can be intense in the sense that it is deeply emotional or insightful. Some persons have experiences which provoke many tears and long prayers. Others take the "leap of faith" (as Kierkegaard suggested) and find great release in having found meaning and purpose for their lives. This is intensely defined as the degree to which a given faith experience affects the intellectual or emotional part of one's personality. There is another aspect of intensity which has to do with the importance of the experience. If a given faith experience causes one to deal with the importance of the experience, if a given faith experience has caused one to return to one's estranged wife or to change vocation or to decide to spend one's income in a new way, then that faith experience has been intense. But not all faith has that much import. It has less effect on one's life patterns. This is not to disparage the experience. It is merely to suggest differences which can be described.

Finally, faith experiences differ in length. They last for varying amounts of time. Some are over in an instant as with a feeling of thanksgiving when one narrowly averts disaster. Others last for days as when a person avidly reads the Gospels and eagerly thinks over their meaning again and again. Experiences that occur at revival meetings often last far beyond the services themselves. Further, an experience may pass quickly, but the decisions made on the basis of it may even last for a lifetime.

So a model for understanding faith experiences should

include the above-mentioned dimensions. They are age, type of emphasis, locale, number of times experience occurs, intensity, and duration. A diagram of this model is given below.

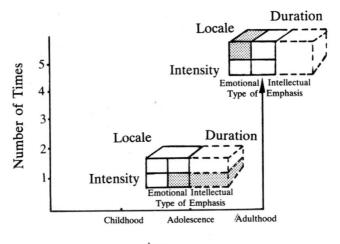

The two blocks drawn in the diagram depict two distinct types of faith experiences that could occur in the same person at different times or in two persons at the same time. The first is an experience in adolescence of a youth who feels deeply moved at a revival meeting to give his heart to God and to serve God in fulltime Christian service. The darkened area indicates this onetime intellectual experience of much intensity which occurs in a group of people is of great importance and has a long-lasting effect. The second is an experience of an adult who attends a weekly Bible study and prayer fellowship. This is a frequent emotional experience in a group setting which lasts only a short time and is of only moderate intensity.

As was said, this model is helpful in understanding the differences in faith experiences between two or more persons at a given time or those experiences occurring at different times within the same person.

This chapter has attempted to describe faith whereas the first chapter defined it and the second chapter explained it. Summing up what has been said, the following statements could be made:

1. Looking from the inside out, faith is always the same. It is a personal response to God which answers the anxieties of life.
2. Looking from the outside in, faith is not always the same by any stretch of the imagination. There are many differences.
3. Abraham was given as an example of the differences in faith experiences that occur within the same person over a lifetime.
4. Whereas faith supposedly deepens and develops over time, it often ebbs and flows. There is such a thing as "falling from grace" and regaining it.
5. The faith experiences of two high-school boys were given as examples of the differences in faith that occur between two persons.
6. A model was given to help in our understanding these differences in the same person from time to time and different persons at the same time.

7. The model includes the following dimensions: age, type of emphasis, locale, frequency, intensity, and duration.

Keeping this model in mind, the next chapter will discuss the results of faith. It is an attempt to answer the question, "What does faith do for us?"

4. The Benefits of Faith

The law of the Lord is perfect, reviving the soul; the testimony of the Lord is sure; making wise the simple; the precepts of the Lord are right, rejoicing the heart; the commandment of the Lord is pure, enlightening the eyes.—Psalm 19:7-8

An experience I had after the death of my father illustrates what faith can do for us. I was only six years old. It was a very frightening time for me. I knew he was very sick, but to be told that he had died was very shocking to me. My mother took me aside and said: "Daddy has gone to be with God. We must live good lives so we can go and be with him someday. In the meantime, he will send his guardian angel to watch over us and take care of us."

Several nights later, I was asleep in the very room where my father had died. I was lonely and scared. I had cried long and hard before going to sleep. Mother had comforted me and had asked God to be present with me through the night. Sometime in the middle of the night, I awoke. I looked around in the darkened room and saw a human form over by the door. At first I was startled and afraid. Then I remembered my mother's words, "He will send his guardian angel to watch over us." The form I saw was the guardian angel. I closed my eyes and went back to sleep, comforted and encouraged. My faith did this for me.

Yes, faith makes things happen. It brings results. Note above the poetic report of the psalmist. Making contact through faith with the law of the Lord revives the soul, makes simple folk wise, bring joy to the heart, and enlightens the eyes. These are psychological or "inside the person" effects of faith. Yes, faith does things *for* us. It has benefits.

That's why we keep seeking faith and allowing it to happen to us. We like its benefits. We remain open to it, and we put ourselves in places where it can happen to us. Faith, thus, becomes a habit; and we continue to pursue it because it has payoffs for us.

Psychologists call these payoffs rewards or reinforcements. They suggest that we do what we do because we are given approval, support, understanding, and direction, i.e., rewards. They conclude that we will cease doing those things for which we are not reinforced by good and positive results. In this sense the act of faith is no different from sailing, studying history, selling insurance, or cleaning house. All must be reinforced or we stop doing them.

Therefore, it is to a discussion of the rewards of faith

that we now turn. It can readily be seen that this is a logical next step based on previous chapters in which

faith was defined as a response of persons to God,
faith was explained as an attempt to meet our basic needs, and
faith was described as the same event experienced in different ways from time to time and from person to person.

Roots and Fruits

William James, the famous psychologist, made the distinction between the *roots* and the *fruits* of religion. This difference is a helpful one to keep in mind as we consider what faith does for us.

The *roots* of faith are those basic needs which provoke our search for God and our openness to him when he comes to us. As listed in chapter 2, these are needs for survival, for satisfaction, for security, and for self-discovery. It will be remembered that these needs are often experienced by us as anxieties about time, about identity, about place, about causality, and about substance. Like the soil in which vegetables are planted, these needs and anxieties are the fertile ground in which faith blooms and grows. They are the roots, the beginnings, the foundations, and the seeds of faith.

The fruits of faith are the results, the payoffs, the rewards, the changes, and the effects that come after the experience itself. Often the outcomes are direct answers to the anxieties we are experiencing. For example, a young man and woman reported they both had accepted Christ as their personal Savior and wanted to be baptized. When asked what the experience meant to them, they reported that they no longer were worried about their sexual relationship and that they felt forgiven for the past. They sensed a new quality to their friendship and felt more able to love each other with a new purpose. Their faith experience was directly applicable to the anxiety or guilt they were experiencing. Many times, this is the case. Faith comes as a clear answer to our concerns about identity, time, place, etc.

At other times, the fruits of faith are less clearly related to our conscious concerns. Something happens to us, but that something is a surprise. It does not appear to relate to any conscious problem we are having, or, if we are experiencing difficulties, it often provides unexpected answers. A friend of mine who had experienced faith at age sixty-five illustrates this type of fruit. He had not been to church for forty years and only attended the Sunday on which his experience occurred out of courtesy to his wife. In the midst of the service, he experienced a profound sense of euphoria, accompanied by a great sense of peace, warmth, emotional aliveness, and joy. It literally changed his life, but in no way was it an answer to any problem or anxiety of which he was aware. He was healthy and successful. It came as a surprise. The fruit was a great blessing, yet the tie to needs and anxieties was unclear.

Thus fruits are the results of faith which sometimes appear as direct answers to anxieties we are experiencing and sometimes come as unexpected surprises apart from any problem we are having. In either case, these fruits are distinct from the roots or origins of faith. These origins or beginnings of faith are the same whether the fruits seem to us clearly related to our anxieties or not. As was said in the last chapter on kinds of faith, all faith is the same no matter where or in whomever it occurs. It is grounded in or begins with needs. Its roots are the same in spite of the fact that the fruits appear different.

How then can we explain that some faith fruits feel like they come out of the blue and are not consciously resolutions of problems we are experiencing? The answer may reside in a model which the anthropologist, Allan Tippett, has proposed.

Tippett's Model of Faith

Tippett suggests that faith experiences follow a pattern which includes several stages. First, there is a period of AWARENESS in which a person is conscious of the possibility that he or she lives in an atmosphere where faith occurs. This is like saying that a person notices the church on the corner or becomes vaguely aware that there are persons who talk about religious experiences they are having. This awareness is often preconscious in that a person would admit to it only with questions such as "Were you aware?" or "Did you notice?" It is much like the background of a painting.

This period of awareness is followed by a point of REALIZATION during which the background of faith becomes the foreground. At this point, persons focus in on those about them who are reporting faith events. Churches, Scriptures, rituals, services, holy persons, etc., all consciously impress the person. This is the time at which one becomes conscious of that which he or she had only been vaguely aware heretofore.

Next, there is a period of DECISION during which,

for the first time, individuals consider the possibility that these faith experiences could be true for them. At this time a person decides to seriously consider the possibility that it could really happen to "me," not just to those about me. The process has moved from vague awareness to conscious realization to a time of serious concentration. Faith has become a possibility.

As might be expected, this period of decision results in a point of ENCOUNTER. This encounter is the faith experience we have been talking about in this book. It is the time at which "it" happens, and one knows from personal experience that God is real. This is the specific point of response to God which we have labeled faith. The shift is from faith as a possibility to faith as an actuality. People report at this point that they, like John Wesley, felt their "hearts strangely warmed and knew their sins forgiven."

Tippett's model continues after his faith point of encounter to a period of INCORPORATION during which the person joins with others in a fellowship of faith. During this time, faith develops, broadens, reoccurs, and becomes a habit. The joy of the encounter of the experience is considered and practiced. The discipline and fellowship of the new group are learned.

This period leads to a point of CONFIRMATION at which an individual publicly states that he or she is a faithing person. This is what most of us know at the time of joining the church. The faith experience has, thus, resulted in a person choosing a new way to live and a new group to which to belong. Finally, there is a period of MATURITY during which a person grows and develops in the life within the faithing fellowship. Recalling the early point of encounter, time and time again, the individual applies the faith to new situations and reexperiences God in different ways and places. One's identity as a person of faith feels solid and comfortable and secure.

The model could be diagramed this way:

Periods

	Awareness	↓	Decision	↓	Incorporation	↓	Maturity
Time							
	Realization		Encounter		Confirmation		

Points

It should be noted that there are four *periods* of time (Awareness, Decision, Incorporation, and Maturity) and there are three *points* in time (Realization, Encounter, and Confirmation). In this book, we have been describing faith experiences as *points in time.* Specifically, we have been considering the encounter point. It is good to note how this point fits into the larger picture of faith development.

Faith at the Conscious and Subconscious Levels

In the description of these periods given above, *awareness* was depicted as a time of vague or preconscious awareness while *decision* was portrayed as a time of clear, considered self-consciousness. Could it be that for the persons for whom faith feels like a surprise that the time of decision goes on beneath their awareness and without their knowing it? If this is so, then we could say the process is the same in both types of faith but that for some people it occurs at a conscious level and for some people it does not. For some, faith comes as a clear answer to anxieties and problems while for others these connections are less obvious, but the relationships are there just the same. Thus, all faith is grounded at its roots in needs, anxieties, and problems. For some persons, these processes go on at a subconscious level, but for other persons they do not. Fruits may be different, but the roots are the same.

William James, with this understanding, has made a distinction between gradual and sudden conversions. He suggested that those for whom conversion was a gradual process were likely to be self-consciously aware of the problem-solving process going on inside them. This eventually leads to the *encounter* out of which faith emerges. He suggested, on the other hand, that those for whom conversion was a sudden experience were likely to be unaware or unconscious of the anxiety laden, problem-solving process going on inside them. They were those who were constitutionally and neurologically able to keep their mental processes supressed. This eventually leads them to the same type of *faith encounter* as the gradual convert. But the onrush of faith into conscious mental life is unexpected and surprising. Their experience of it as unconnected to anxiety is due to their ability to keep parts of their mental life separate from each other.

Thus it can be said that the roots of faith are the same for all persons. However, the fruits or results vary. A description of these fruits follows.

The Fruits of Faith for Children and Youth
A way of looking at what faith does for children and youth has been suggested by David Elkind. He proposes

that four distinct lifelong needs appear during infancy, early childhood, childhood, and adolescence. Faith provides answers to these needs or "searches" as he terms them.

The first search is for performance. Knowing that the world does not go away when we shut our eyes is a foregone conclusion for most of us. We do not stop to realize that the infant had to *acquire* this sense of people and things. It is a developmental accomplishment. The major problem which all persons must face, however, is that people are not permanent. Their loved ones die. Faith offers a solution to this dilemma. By trusting God, the individual resolves the problem of permanence. God transcends time, space, and physical matter. He comes to us as the One who will not pass away, and he promises to conserve us and our loved ones in his eternal care. The first fruit of faith is a sense of trust in God to preserve us.

The second search is for the *right words*. In early childhood, the child learns his or her language. The excitement of a young child learning the names of things about him/her is awesome! This search for names continues throughout life. As experience becomes more complex, the task often includes the use of symbols or signs. When people realize there is more to life than everyday appearances, the job becomes even more difficult. Being able to name something reduces anxiety and makes relationships possible. Remember the words of Moses at the burning bush: "[If] they ask me 'What is his name?' what shall I say to them?" And the reply of God was "Say this to the people of Israel, 'The Lord, the God of your fathers, the God of Abraham, the God of Isaac, and the God of Jacob, has sent me to you': this is my name for ever (Exodus 3:13–15). When we have a faith experience then God has a name. God becomes friendly and identifiable. The unknown is made known. The lifelong search for a name for the mysterious and the transcendent is over.

Third, the search for *relations* is the typical problem of childhood. In this part of life, school is the dominant force. And the prime message of school is to put things in proper relationship to each other. The child is intrigued with learning how things work, what they are made of, and to what use they can be put. Integral to this is the search for how one relates to this world of objects and persons. Even more puzzling is "Who am I in relation to the cosmos, to the transcendent, or to God?" Faith offers an answer to this question. In coming to accept the truths which we have always heard, we come to know who we really are. The Christian truth that people are deeply loved children of God becomes a personal reality that settles our search for relations. We have an identity that cannot be taken away from us.

Last, there is the search for *order* during the adolescent years. Here, for the first time, persons are able to look for underlying principles which hold diverse facts and different historical periods together. Here, for the first time, persons realize they, too, are in history and that they need to feel a part of ideals and movements that transcend the moment. Faith, once again, provides the ultimate answer to this search. We feel attached to that which underlies the change of every day. Through worship and trust, we witness to an acceptance of meaning in spite of confusion and fluctuation. Thus, the search for trustful order and purpose is ended through faith.

These are the four fruits of faith from Elkind's point of view. They are developmental searches which appear at certain times in life but continue throughout life. The infant, child, and youth who have faith experiences settle these searches in ways that will continue to benefit them throughout their lives. The need to find permanence, identity, words for the mysterious, and underlying truths in life—all these continue. But these needs can be met over and over again through faith. Thus the fruits of faith, from this point of view, are knowing that God will not leave us, that he is who he said he was in Christ, that we can rest peacefully in our identities as his children, and that he has an underlying purpose which governs the world.

Let us turn to another model of fruits. This one was proposed by William James, whom we have mentioned before.

The Fruits of Faith for Adults

William James has suggested several fruits of faith for adults. However, these effects are probably just as true for adolescents as well. They are characteristic of most faith experiences which date from the traditional age of accountability, i.e., about twelve years old.

The rewards of religious experience can come to us at three stages of development. These stages are similar to Tippett's periods of *decision, incorporation,* and *maturity* which we discussed earlier in this chapter. James calls them the Conversion state, the Assurance state, and the

Transformation state. Faith does different things for us at each different point.

In the *conversion state* or *decision period,* there results a joyous feeling that a struggle has been resolved and that peace has been achieved. It is a joyous, warm sense of contentment and aliveness. Many of us can attest to such emotions. Most often they are more feelings than thoughts. We can recall and reexperience them in memory. Like Tolstoy we can agree, "The light has never wholly died away."

In the *assurance state* or *incorporation period,* several things happen to us as a result of our faith experiences. Initially, we find ourselves free from worry and willing to be ourselves even though the environment remains the same. Worry and striving are gone. We feel content with God's grace and presence. There is a sense of certainty that pervades our daily lives. Jonathan Edwards called it an inner sweetness down, deep within us. Many of us would agree with this description of the feeling.

The second fruit of faith during this *assurance state* is a sense that we have a new knowledge which we did not have before. Here we put thoughts to our feelings. We use the words of faith in a different sense than ever before. We feel enlightened. It is like reaching a point of awareness. We exclaim "Ah ha! Now I see it." At this time we know the answers we have are true. We have a sense of knowing something we never knew before.

Third, the world around us looks different during this assurance state of faith. Things attract us which seemed mundane or repulsive before. There is a beauty to the world and our circumstances which had not been there before. Things have changed in a surprising way. We see through new eyes in an intriguing and amazing manner. As one man said, "Oh, how I was changed . . . everything became new. My horses and my hogs and everybody seemed changed." Many could agree with this description.

The *state of transformation* is called by Tippett the Period of Maturity during which faith experiences result in a deepening of life and a change of character. James suggests four fruits of faith during this time. The first effect is that we become aware of God's purpose for the world over and beyond our own self-interests.

We have another sense of knowing something new for the first time. We become exhilarated with the awareness that God is at work all about us in many ways and that this is as important as the personal work he has accomplished in our own salvation.

The second effect is a sense of friendliness of this powerful God of the universe. We experience his desire that we become part of his plan and purpose. Thus, we willingly surrender ourselves to him. It is this feeling of self-surrender and of a willingness to be used by God that permeates faith experiences during this time. The admonition of Paul to "present your bodies as living sacrifices" (Romans 12:1) becomes a live possibility for us. Many of us know this effect to be a reality.

Third, this self-surrender brings with it newer feelings of elation and freedom than we have ever known before. These are more sublime emotions than the peace and contentment of our conversion. They are feelings which tell us we are stronger and more dedicated than we were. They are emotions similar to the invigoration we feel when we tackle a job with enthusiasm. Many of us can attest to this excitement in our faith experience.

Last, this *state of transformation* results in a shifting of our concern from self to others. We freely say yes to the needs of those near and far. There is a definite increase in charity toward, tenderness about, and sympathy for the less fortunate. This is the culmination of the awareness of God's purpose and our sense of self-surrender to his work. Other people become important to us, and their welfare becomes our concern. Charity and brotherly love become dominant in our thoughts and feelings. Many of us could report experiencing these new unselfish attitudes.

So, these are the fruits of faith for adolescents and adults as conceived by William James. They describe the effects that occur during *conversion, assurance,* and *transformation states.* They begin with a sense of peace and end with a commitment to helping others.

To sum up what faith can do *for* us, this chapter has suggested:

1. All faith is grounded in or results from our efforts to meet basic needs. These are the roots of our faith.

2. Faith has certain results, rewards, or effects that are tied to our basic needs. These are the fruits of faith.

3. For some of us, the fruits of faith seem clearly related to anxieties or problems we are facing. For others of us, faith's fruits come as a surprise.

4. Whether we realize it or not, all the fruits of faith are connected to our needs, anxieties, or problems. In

some of us the process can go on at a subconscious level. Thus, we are not aware of it.

5. Faith can have the following results for us as children and adolescents: End our search for permanence, for a name for God, for identity, and for purpose.

6. As adults, faith can give us joyous peace, freedom from worry, contentment with circumstances, new knowledge about the meaning of life, new perception of the world about us, awareness of God's purpose in the world, a willingness to surrender ourselves to him, freedom, enthusiasm, and a feeling of unselfishness.

Just as faith can do some things *for* us, so it can do some things *to* us. The next chapter will discuss these.

5. The Dangers of Faith

Woe to you, scribes and Pharisees, hypocrites! for you tithe mint and dill and communin, and have neglected the weightier matters of the law, justice and mercy and faith; . . . for you cleanse the outside of the cup and of the plate but inside they are full of extortion and rapacity. . . . for you are like whitewashed tombs, which outwardly appear beautiful, but within they are full of dead men's bones and all uncleanness. So you also outwardly appear righteous to men, but within you are full of hypocrisy and iniquity—(Matthew 23:23, 25, 27-28).

Gestalt psychologists make the distinction between what a given behavior does *for* us and what it does *to* us. They suggest that while we get something out of the things we do, we also pay a price. And so it is with faith. Faith has its benefits. It also has its dangers. In the last chapter, we discussed the *good* fruits of faith. In this chapter we will discuss those that are *bad*. We will consider what faith can do *to* us.

A good starting point is the words of Jesus noted above. Here Jesus is talking to the religious leaders of his day—those who probably had experienced faith more often than anyone else. Yet something had happened to them. They seemed to have substituted outer behavior for inner experience. One of the effects of faith that was not mentioned in the last chapter is that persons tend to become active participants in religious groups after their experiences. This happens during the Period of Incorporation as Tippett described it. People are incorporated or brought into or become active members of churches and fellowships. They learn the way those groups express their faith. They worship and witness according to the customs of the groups they are in. Many of the good fruits mentioned in the last chapter are channeled through group activities. Churches provide ways for people to surrender themselves to God's ways and to show their unselfishness to others. This is good and necessary.

Danger 1—Outer Behavior Replaces Inner Experience

That which is good can become bad if persons substitute outer behavior for inner experience. The scribes and Pharisees were like that. Jesus suggested they give 10 percent of their goods to God even down to the spices in their food. They were scrupulous in these minute details, but forgot the weightier or more important laws, such as justice and mercy. These are part of the fruits of faith William James wrote about (see the last chapter) when he said that we come to a new sense of God's purpose in the world and of our place in it. The religious leaders of Jesus' day had lost the inner experience of faith and had put a set of outer behaviors in its place.

This, then, is the first thing faith can do to us: It can delude us into thinking that a behavior substitutes for inner experience. Worshiping, attending church meetings, practicing holy habits like tithing, Bible reading, and praying—all these can trick us into ignoring the more important issues. These "weightier matters," as Jesus called them, are our inner sense of God's purpose and our need to be unselfishly concerned with justice and mercy.

Psychologists know how easy it is to learn to do some task and then forget its real meaning. This loss of understanding can be seen in workers on an assembly line who forget they are building a car and even distract themselves intentionally so that they will not become bored. Another example is the violin player in the symphony orchestra who plays the symphony faultlessly but lifelessly because he or she has blocked out the meaning for the event. So it is with faith. We all know persons who seem to be going through the motions of religious living. They seem to have lost heart and are just going through the motions. This is a real danger in faith.

Even worse, we can come to the place where the real reward for us is the attention we get from others. We tend to forget the value of the inner experience which initially brought us into this faithing way of life. Jesus noted this when he advised, "Beware of practicing your piety before men in order to be seen of them; for then you will have no reward from your Father who is in heaven" (Matthew 6:1). He illustrates this by talking about those who make a commotion when they give offerings and stand on the street corners when they pray. In both cases the people were more interested in impressing others than in expressing their inner faith.

Gordon Allport, the late well-known psychologist, called this the difference between an intrinsic and an extrinsic orientation to religion. The extrinsically oriented person is more interested in being known by others as a religious person than in personal spiritual development. The intrinsically oriented person cares less about what others think and is more interested in witnessing to the experience inside when he or she worships in public.

So the first thing that faith can do *to* us is to divert our attention from inner experience to outer behavior. It is easy to discover suddenly that we care more about what others think of us than we do about those deep emotions and insights which are the true rewards of faith.

Danger 2—Pretending We Are Something We Are Not

Another issue is that faith experiences inspire us to change our lives. Many of the fruits of faith mentioned in the last chapter speak to this end. We feel different, and we want to act differently. We often tell others about our experiences, and they expect us to show that it matters. But change is difficult, and we all know it. The following anonymous poem humorously attests to this fact:

The sermon now ended, each turned and descended.
The eels went on eeling, the peels went on peeling.
Much delighted were they, but preferred the old way.

I suspect that is what happened to the scribes and Pharisees. They probably started out delighted and enthused by their faith experiences. However, they found it difficult to really change. They, then, found it easy to pretend their lives were transformed by acting religiously and by talking about their experience. Finally, they came to the place where they were no longer having faith experiences nor were they any different than they had been before. Jesus described them as cups that were clean on the outside but still dirty on the inside. He further spoke of them as tombs which were exquisite on the outside but full of dead men's bones on the inside. The word we often hear used for this state is "hypocrite."

Psychologists know how easy it is to become a hypocrite. This is particularly true when persons claim they have had an earthshaking experience that has changed their lives. They expect great changes to occur within themselves, and others begin to look for them too. But change is hard, and having to admit failure is difficult. Very often persons turn to hypocrisy. They simply pretend. However, they don't get away with it because other people see through the illusion. This is sad. How many times have we heard someone say, "All church members are hypocrites"? Many of them are. Perhaps it would be better to admit our frailty and weakness than to pretend we are what we are not. For it is probably true, as the theologian Karl Barth reportedly said, that there is really no difference between persons inside the church and those outside it—all are forgiven sinners. Those inside the church know it, while those outside the church do not.

Danger 3—Becoming Lazy and Feeling No Pressure to Do Good.

This unconcern for righteousness was the prime reason Sigmund Freud was so critical of Christianity. He saw many Christians in Vienna who were prejudiced against Jews and who made no effort to right the injustices of the day. He felt most of what he saw was a childish reliance on a forgiving God. He did not think Christians were concerned with issues of justice and mercy, because he felt their God did not require them to be righteous in order to be saved. He suggested that Christians should give up their childish beliefs in God and grow up. Then they could take their place among those who were working for the good of all. Freud did not realize that the lethargy he saw was a distortion of faith, not one of its intended fruits.

The writer of the Letter of James pointed to the truth that while God accepts us as we are, he fully intends that we will join him in the task of good and godly work.

> What does it profit, my brethren, if a man says he has faith but has not works? Can his faith save him? If a brother or sister is ill-clad and in lack of daily food, and one of you says to them, "Go in peace, be warmed and filled," without giving them the things needed for the body, what does it profit? So faith, by itself, if it has no works, is dead (James 2:14-17).

Thus, one thing that faith can do to us when or if it does not provoke in us an enthusiastic and energetic dedication to good works, is to make our faith die.

There are some psychologists (for example, O.

Hobart Mowrer), who believe that mental illness can be caused by accepting God's forgiveness without feeling any obligation to do good deeds. He calls this a weakness of conscience that sets up a deep-seated guilt inside persons. This guilt can become troublesome and can actually cause people to have emotional and mental breakdowns. They cannot live with the realization that they have not let their faith experiences evoke ethical behavior from them. Thus, from Mowrer's point of view, mental illness is due to guilt and can be healed by confession and atonement.

Mowrer himself is a witness to this understanding of the danger of feeling no pressure to perform. He was hospitalized in a mental hospital for depression. He did not seem to be getting better in spite of good treatment from the hospital staff. One day, some visiting Christians told him that if he would repent of his sins, he would get well. On his next visit home, he stood up in church, confessed his sins, and reported his willingness to make right his wrongdoings. He immediately began to get better.

Today, Mowrer advocates "integrity" therapy which is treatment based on encouraging people to admit their guilt for doing wrong or for doing nothing. This treatment encourages them to get busy doing good. It states "Only by facing guilt directly and by becoming active in atoning for one's sin can good mental health result."

There is the constant danger that our trust in a forgiving God can lull us to sleep and keep us from the advanced benefits of faith which are self-surrender to God and active involvement in his work. Faith can make us lazy. If we are not careful, we will not feel the pressure to perform.

Danger 4—Intolerance of Those Who Are Different

Another bad fruit of faith experiences can be a growing intolerance of those who are different. This can range from a disrespect of those whose religion is not the same as ours to a discount of those fellow Christians who have different ways of praying than we do. It can be as subtle as a lack of appreciation for the ways other people worship or it can be as blatant as a dislike of Jews because their forefathers rejected Jesus. It can be as specific as a distrust of those who baptize differently or as general as a suspicion of those who call them conservative or liberal.

This phenomenon is very familiar and understandable to psychologists. It is a tendency known by a variety of names. Some of these terms are authoritarianism, closed-mindedness, prejudice, and intolerance. The underlying dynamic can be explained by a process called cognitive-dissonance. In cognitive-dissonance (or doubt) persons can feel a need to strengthen a decision once they have made it. Therefore, they try to reduce whatever questions they have or doubts they are feeling by rationalizing their decision. They do this by thinking up reasons for their position. This is followed by arguments against other alternatives. This process makes them feel more comfortable with what they have decided to do.

It is not strange at all that this process of cognitive-dissonance should go on after faith experiences. After all, having faith does stretch our minds. We feel a need to justify such an outlandish event as having contact with Almighty God. It goes far beyond everyday experience. We need all the help we can muster to make it palatable to us. Therefore, it is understandable that we try hard to reduce our insecurity after faith experiences. And it is during this period that we run the greatest risk of becoming intolerant, authoritarian, closed-minded, and prejudiced.

Much research has shown that there is a definite tendency for many religious persons to be prejudiced against persons of other races in spite of the fact that theirs is a religion of brotherly love. They tend to support prayer and Bible reading in public institutions even when it offends nonreligious persons. They tend to be authoritarian in child-rearing practices, pro status quo in labor-management relations, and resistive toward the rights of minorities. It seems as if the inclination to think in black and white can be generalized in many attitudes other than religion.

Thus, faith experiences can cause us, in terms of transactional analysis, to take a chronic "I'm OK— You're not OK" position in life. It can be a general attitude toward all non-Christians or a specific attitude toward other Christians who are not just like us. In fact, it sometimes seems as if some Christians look on other Christians more as enemies than as brothers. Further, this tendency can cause Christians to forget their heritage in the Jewish faith. A suggestive antidote to this attitude was seen recently on a bumpersticker. In answer to the somewhat presumptuous claim of "I found it," this bumpersticker (on a Jewish car) simply said, "We never lost it!"

So becoming intolerant of those who are different is yet another thing that can happen to us if we are not careful. No doubt these are bad effects nourished in shallow and distorted experiences. Nevertheless, they can be avoided only through much effort.

Danger 5—Getting Too Much of a Good Thing

The final bad effect faith experiences can have on us is to make us become fanatics. We can get too much of a good thing. As William James said we can carry religious living to a "convulsive extreme." These are strong words. They suggest a condition in which persons become consumed with their religion and are obsessed with their faith. We have all experienced such people. They often use a lot of "God talk" and report every decision they make as being "the will of God" for them. Sometimes they spend all their spare time at church to the neglect of their families. They pray and read their Bibles so much that they do not have time for their work or play. On other occasions, they persist in trying to convert others to their point of view. Or they scrupulously avoid contact with whatever they consider evil, whether it be a person or a place or certain foods or thoughts. Many are narrowminded and opinionated, while others are pushovers for con men. Sometimes they are so radical they give their money away and neglect their health. They seem to spend their time on causes that more practical people evaluate as failures.

Psychologists can easily understand how faith experiences tempt folks to become fanatics. If we take seriously what happens to us in faith, we see the world with new eyes, and we feel strongly about God's will for us. These are the benefits of faith we can expect if we give ourselves over to God. They enrich, enliven, and change us if we let them. And in almost every case, faith alters the way we look at life. It changes our values and causes us to think again about what is important to us. There is the great temptation to follow our faith experiences into excessive asceticism, devotionalism, excessive piety, and self-deprecation. At the extremes, this would mean giving up what we have and taking up an entirely new lifestyle that we felt was in keeping with God's will. Jesus even encouraged this in his words to the rich, young ruler, "Go, sell what you have, and give to the poor, and . . . follow me" (Mark 10:21). He further stated "He who loves father or mother more than me is not worthy of me" (Matthew 10:37). The implication is that we are to radically change our lives when we become faithing persons. Jesus even implies that our reluctance to do this may keep us out of the kingdom of heaven.

From this point of view, fanaticism may be a more positive benefit rather than a danger of faith. While there may be a need for "saints" in the sum of things, the average person has to stay in the world at the same time he or she maintains contact with God through faith experiences. As the business owner said to Tom Rath in *The Man in the Gray Flannel Suit,* "Somebody has to give his or her life to this business." Tom had just said that he did not want to take work home at night or on weekends, that he wanted a life of his own, that he did not want to give himself for the company. But most of us do have to give our lives to this-worldly concerns. We must stay here while we experience God in faith. The average person cannot give it all up to enter a monastery or otherworldly self-denying vocation. Thus fanaticism for us is probably more a danger than a benefit.

I am not encouraging Aristotle's Golden Mean—"moderation in all things." I am not saying that too much religion is a bad thing. Nor am I suggesting that we should keep our faith under control and not let it get out of hand. I do think I'm saying that saintliness is for the few. We should think carefully when we feel tempted to turn our backs on our environment or become so possessed with certain words, ideas, or experiences that we forget that we must continue to live in a situation where daily work is to be done and where we must have our prime influence by communicating with those about us. It is a delicate balance that probably must be worked out by each individual with much prayer and thought. It is possible to take faith seriously without becoming a fanatic, but it is a difficult task.

More importantly, the Christian faith has always been tempted to become an otherworldly preoccupation. However, from earliest times this tendency has been rejected. There were those in apostolic times who wanted to think of faith as a way to get beyond this evil world and to achieve supernatural and otherworldly insight. They rejected this world as evil and said the Christian's main task was to live for heaven. The church said no to this. In the Apostle's Creed, we read the answer: God is "maker of heaven and of earth." God is not simply the God of heaven. He made earth as well. He is not fighting with a lesser god who rules the earth. No, this is his world. It is the good earth, because it is God's earth. We are to affirm the world and try to live lives of faith within it for its own sake. The Christian faith is not an Eastern faith like Hinduism or Buddhism. They emphasize self-denial and individual enlightenment. They advocate rising above preoccupation with this earth. But the Christian faith is concerned with earth as well as heaven. That is why fanaticism that leads to separation from the world or rejection of it is a danger that should be avoided.

So the last of the things faith can do *to* us is to provoke us to fanaticism in which we become obsessed with religion and forget the world around us.

This chapter has described five dangers that faith can do *to* us. They are the dangers of faith.

1. The first danger was that we will replace inner experience with outer behavior.
2. The second danger was that we will pretend we are something we are not.
3. The third danger was that we will become lazy and feel no pressure to perform.
4. The fourth danger was that we will become intolerant of those who are different from us.
5. The fifth danger was that we will become fanatics.

In comparison to the last chapter where the good results of faith were described, this chapter has listed those side effects that were negative, bad, or dangerous. They are to be avoided and guarded against if at all possible.

The next chapter will be concerned with the future of faith in our lives.

6. What Can We Expect of Faith in Our Futures?

The Lord is my shepherd, I shall not want; he makes me lie down in green pastures. He leads me beside still waters; he restores my soul.— (Psalm 23:1-2).

So far in this book we have considered what *has happened* to us. We have discussed the meaning of our faith, the various types of faith, the benefits of faith, and even the dangers of faith. In this chapter we will think about *what will happen to us.* What is the future of faith in our lives?

Psalm 23 speaks about this issue in a poetic but insightful way. The psalmist combines what is with what will be. Note the words:

What is	*What will be*
The Lord is my shepherd,	I shall not want;
He makes me lie down in green pastures,	
He leads me beside still waters;	
He restores my soul.	Even though I walk
He leads me in paths of right-eousness for his name's sake.	through the valley of the shadow of death, I fear no evil;

for thou art with me; thy rod and thy staff,
   they comfort me.

Thou preparest a table before me in the presence of my enemies; thou anointest my head with oil, my cup overflows.	Surely goodness and mercy shall follow me all the days of my life; and I shall dwell in the house of the Lord for ever.

The writer seems to suggest that the future can be predicted on the basis of the past. What God has done he will continue to do. Or speaking from the individual's point of view, "I will continue to experience God in the future in the same way I have known him in the past." Moreover, "I will know him as shepherd then just as I know him as a shepherd now."

The Future Equals the Past

In other words, we can predict the future from the past. This will sound simplistic, but it is not meant to be so. Many of us have applied this maxim about the future being built on the past to many parts of our lives. But we may rarely think of it in reference to our religious experience. Just as we can use our past experience to predict how much time it will take to drive from Chicago to Indianapolis, whether hamburgers will cook over charcoal, which type of music we will prefer, or when a mail order package will arrive from a firm in Philadelphia, so we can estimate with some assurance that a given pattern of faith events which occurred once will occur again. This may seem a bit exaggerated, but it is generally true. Persons have failed to realize how predictable God is and how reliable our experience of him becomes. Thus, the confidence that we can expect faith in the future to be like faith in the past implies something about God and something about people.

On the one hand, the Bible speaks again and again about God's faithfulness (Psalm 25:10) and his steadfast love (Psalm 138:8). God never changes (Malachi 3:6), which means he is always available and is constantly coming toward us. In fact, he has arrived and is ever present with us. As the scripture says, "and his name shall be called Emmanuel (which means, God with us)" (Matthew 1:23). So the truth about God is that the future will be as reliable as the past. In this we can put our trust. In fact, that is what the Christian hope is all about. It says that we will not be surprised in the future. What we know of God now will be true of him in time to come. As far as God is concerned, we can always experience him because he will always be available.

On the other hand, this relationship of the future to the past implies something about persons. Psychologists, whose job it is to study behavior, know that people are creatures of habit. There are many ways to live a life. Cultural differences are colorful evidence of this. However, within a culture and across a lifetime most individuals evidence little change in the ways they dress, spend their time, eat their food, or do their work. People become habituated. They fall into patterns. So psychologists assume that if they can know enough about a person's past they can, with some assurance, predict the future. If we know one, we can predict the other.

Many illustrations come to mind. A friend of mine said, "I always get goosepimples when I take the bread at the service of Holy Communion." Another friend reported, "I never see a sunset that I don't feel the presence of God." Again, one of my in-laws becomes teary-eyed everytime he sings "What a Friend We Have in Jesus." It is the song he remembers his mother singing so often. Others have said, "Whenever I read Romans 8 or hear the *Messiah* or pray in my car or hear a moving sermon or visit a cathedral or share deeply with my friends, I have a religious experience." The list could go on and on.

If these unique whenevers or alwayses are known for a particular person, then it can be foretold with some assurance that he or she will experience God in much the same way.

This is the law of habit. Although we could experience God in a wide variety of ways (just as we could eat numerous foods), we, nevertheless, experience him in only a limited manner (just as we grow to prefer only a particular selection of things to eat). We are, indeed, creatures of habit. Our habits are the filters we develop to bring order to our world and to make things predictable. And so it is with faith. Although situations will change, we may grow old, our children will leave, and we may even live in a new house—yet our faith habits will stand us in good stead. In most cases, our experience of God can be the same, if we let it.

This could be diagramed as follows:

Religious Experience in the Past

Past religious experience

to

Response 1————————————Situation 1

(a habit we learn)

Present Religious Experience

to

Response 1————————————Situation 2

(a habit we apply)

This has been called by the psychologists of learning "pure generalization." It includes responding to the present by doing what one did in the past. Very, very often it works.

By responding to God as we always have, we experience him once again in spite of the fact that we are older and times have changed.

Reclaiming the Old

Our experience of God can be the same—if we let it. This suggests that the future cannot always be predicted from the past. We all know what it is to lose the vital emotional content of an experience. We may remember the event, but the original feeling is replaced by a longing, a sense of nostalgia for what once was and no longer seems to be. Our habits seem to sometimes fail us.

In fact, the fear of not being able to maintain a vital and lively faith led to the writing of this chapter. Even those who have had rich, strong, and frequent religious experiences in the past have been heard to say:

"Church just isn't what it used to be . . . " *or*

"When I was a teen-ager, we used to have a big bonfire, *and*

I was very conscious of God's presence; but today . . ." *or*

"I used to be deeply stirred by the choir, but not anymore . . . " *or*

"I used to work hard for the Lord, but I seem to have lost my enthusiasm . . . " *or*

"Since my children have grown up, I find it hard to get any meaning out of praying—we used to do it together . . . " *or*

"Something has changed. . . . I just don't get excited like I used to get. . . . I can't seem to make contact with God anymore. . . ."

These are very familiar complaints. St. John of the Cross, medieval mystic, called such experiences "the dark night of the soul." He said it felt like God had deserted him. In all cases, the past experience ought to make the future predictable—but it does not. How can this be explained?

One answer to this question may lie in the old adage "You can get too much of a good thing." This is paradoxical in light of the assertion that how one met God in the past ought to predict best how one will meet him in the future. However, as was noted in the list of the dangers of faith, even faith habits can deteriorate to the point where one continues to go through the motions but loses the inner excitement.

This can be a slow, almost imperceptible process. Suddenly one becomes aware that it has been going on for a long time—faith has been losing its vitality and its excitement. Often this awareness occurs when circumstances change. For example, we often realize that we have lost a sense of God's presence when a loved one dies or a person goes away to college or a friend moves away or a new minister comes to the church. One discovers in these times that what once was stimulating or evocative no longer works.

Psychologists call this the subtle shift from inner to outer motivation. That which used to serve an inner need over time comes to meet an outer need. While the universal inner motive is to reduce one's anxiety, the outer need is to be comfortable in one's environment. The individual's way of experiencing God in his or her unique situation often meets that need. After a while, being comfortable with the environment comes to suffice for experience with God. When the situation changes, however, the truth comes out. As the individual tries again to relate to God in the old way, there is the feeling that something is missing. The person has become accustomed to outer comfort and has substituted it for inner experience. When the circumstances change, the effort to reclaim the original enthusiasm is not successful. There had been too much of a good thing, and its meaning was lost by relying too much on the environment to give peace.

How can the original religious experience be reclaimed? Note that the question was not "Can the original experience be reclaimed?" because I have no doubt that it can. The issue is "how" not "whether." First, a person can acknowledge that the situation today is different than it was yesterday, and that more than likely this change in outer environment is what is causing the sense of loss and discomfort. Admitting that one substituted outer for inner rewards is simply admitting one is human. Most of us do it. However, if we do not acknowledge this, we may persist in our frustration and even become angry thinking it is God who has abandoned us. Second, admitting this has happened leaves us free to make the old response to a new situation. That is, we can engage in the old religious experience without expecting the same environmental support that we used to receive. And this leaves us free to reexperience what started the religious habit to begin with. Further, it allows us to look for new, but different, dimensions of the old faith event.

An illustration will clarify this point. My mother used to read stories to me from *Hurlbut's Story of the Bible*. They were beautiful and inspiring. I grew to love the stories and the time I spent in her lap while she was reading to me. Sometime later I tried to recapture that feeling by reading these same stories to my young sons. It never felt the same. I soon stopped reading. More recently, however, I have begun to read the stories again. My mother is long deceased, and I am now at mid-life. Yet, I have often felt very warmed and enthused as I read those very familiar stories, thought of her, and allowed God to speak to me in the present moment. I am immensely stirred by the stories of Abraham, Joseph, and David. I have reclaimed this religious experience for myself even though I can no longer obtain the comfort of my mother's presence.

This is what psychologists of learning call "generalization." I have made an old response to a new situation. This means that I have responded in an old, familiar, habitual way to a new set of stimuli and by doing so have found reinforcements similar to those I received when I used to hear the stories read by my mother. The event could be diagramed as follows:

> Original Religious Experience
> to
> Response ———————Situation
> 1   (old habit)
> Reclaimed Religious Experience
> to
> Response ———————Situation
> 1a   (old habit slightly
>   changed)

The original behavior was listening (and eventually helping to read) stories from *Hurlbut's Story of the Bible.* This was a very early religious experience for me. The reclaimed behavior was reading these same stories by myself in my living room and having a similar heartwarming religious experience even though my mother is dead, and I can no longer hear her read to me.

Being Open to the New

Of course, another way to reclaim the old religious experience is to simply remember it for what it was and cultivate a new type of faith entirely. This is tantamount to "Reclaim it by not reclaiming it." Just let it be and treasure it in memory. "Give yourself permission not to have to always be or feel the same as you once did" could be the admonition. "Remember it, but do not strain yourself to recapture it" would be another piece of good advice from this point of view.

This approach makes good sense. For example, a friend of mine played his last set of tennis when he was fifty-seven years old. He is now eighty. He would not think of playing tennis nowadays. His health won't allow it. But he remembers enthusiastically and recounts avidly the experiences during the years when he did play. So it is with faith. We all have a treasury of past experiences. We no longer do these things, but we can remember them.

Listening as Mother reads stories to us;
Going to summer camp and sitting by bonfires;
Studying the formation of the Bible and no longer thinking of God as an old man up there;
Missing our children who are married and our loved ones who are far away;
Realizing the choir is not as good;
Having the minister change pastorates; or
Having friends move away.

And memory is probably the most precious gift God has placed in our minds. It ties the present with the past. It makes possible a type of reexperience that is not bound by time or space.

This leaves us free for the present. We do not strain

ourselves to make today over in terms of the past. We let the past be the past. Thus we are free to let the present be the present. We can be open to new religious experience. This could be diagramed as follows:

Religious Experience in the Past
to
Response 1 ——————— Situation 1
(remembered and cherished)

Religious Experience in the Present
to
Response 2 ——————— Situation 2
(new and unique to the present)

An old maxim suggests you can't teach an old dog new tricks. Yet we are not talking about dogs. We are talking about persons, and persons can be taught new tricks. While they are creatures of habits, they are not slaves to habits. Faith can change with the times. God can be experienced in new ways because he is God, not some static entity who goes and comes.

This makes good sense in light of the model this book has proposed. Religious experience meets our anxieties about life.

One's anxieties change over the life-span. They take on different forms dependent on whether we are facing the dilemmas of childhood, adolescence, young adulthood, mid-adulthood, or late adulthood. The anxieties of a young person seeking a vocation or deciding whom to marry are different from those of a retiree or a person whose mate has just died. So it is hoped that religious experience will change with the situation a person is facing at a given point in life. This is to say, the religion of childhood should be different from the religion of mid-adulthood. The life pedicaments are different.

In order for new religious experience to occur, however, a person must be open, and that means being free and expectant. One must be free in the sense of not being bound by old habits in such a manner that one is blind to new ways in which God would make contact with him or her. One must be expectant in the sense that a person actually goes out looking for God and anticipates that he will be there.

I remember the first year my wife and I were away from the situation in which we had grown up and the region of the country in which we had always lived. We were in graduate shool in a strange environment. The first several Sundays, we sought out what was familiar to us. We attended the nearby United Methodist Church, which was the denomination to which we were accustomed. Thereafter, however, we periodically attended a Buddhist temple, a Greek Orthodox, a Roman Catholic, and a Pentecostal church. I recall the priest standing at the door of the Greek Orthodox sanctuary pinching off hunks of cake and passing them to us with these words, "The body of Christ for your life." It brought chills to my skin. It was very moving. I was open to new religious experience.

But openness does not always mean expectancy. We can be tolerant with many other expressions of faith but not look for anything to happen to us. As we grow up and grow older there is a decided tendency to become close-minded to other types of faith experience than those to which we are accustomed. Expectancy is an intentional mind-set that indicates we are ready to receive something new when it comes.

The shepherds in Luke 2 are prime examples of this. They have been depicted as persons who were surprised by God in the midst of tending their sheep. They would never have stopped their sheepherding and gone to Bethlehem had they not been open to distraction and novelty. But more than that, they were expectant. We have every right to believe that these were no ordinary shepherds. They were Hebrews—part of the children of Israel. They, like their kinsmen, were looking for the Messiah. They expected him to come and were anticipating his arrival. Thus, a combination of openness and expectation made it possible for them to experience God in a surprising and unique manner.

It would seem, therefore, that faith has a future among those who are open and expectant. Although most of the research on religious experience suggests that adolescence is the typical time for conversion, there is more to faith than conversion. Persons of all ages and at different times within life can experience God in a variety of manners which are not definable under the term conversion. Those old-timers who used to tell about their religious experience as if it were a once-in-a-lifetime affair are exceptions. Astonishing things can occur in the face of new situations—if persons are willing and hopeful.

An illustration of one of the possibilities for new religious experience is the Life in the Spirit seminar, a course offered in many Roman Catholic parishes. In this seminar, persons who desire to acquire gifts of the Spirit are invited to come together for study and practice.

After several weeks of investigation into the biblical and theological understanding of the gifts of the Holy Spirit, the participants are blessed by the laying on of hands. As prayers are offered each participant receives the Holy Spirit and attempts to express it in some way. The typical way is through the gift of speaking in tongues. No one of the participants has expressed their faith in this way before. They come to the class in an open and expectant manner. Their interest is usually rewarded by a novel religious experience in which they surrender their minds to God, and they pray in words that sound like foreign languages. This is a good example of how adults at mid-life seek out new ways to express their faith.

The Bible says to us "Ask, and it will be given you, seek and you will find, knock and it will be opened to you" (Matthew 7:7). No doubt this suggestion by Jesus is an admonition to keep pursuing our faith throughout our lives. It is an encouragement to never let our religious experience grow stale. It is a promise that we will find what we are looking for. God will not disappoint our search.

It has been said by psychologists of religion that the present generation is one that is seeking for experience. Dogmas and rituals will not suffice unless they evoke a subjective sense of reality, vitality, and enthusiasm. Our day, therefore, is one in which persons are sensitive to their need for faith experiences which will permeate their whole existence and make them feel alive.

This is not a new idea. The late famous psychologist Abraham Maslow wrote of our great need to actualize ourselves through peak experiences. Of all the peak experiences available to people, Maslow felt that religious experiences offered the most rewards. In fact religion, for him, was synonymous with ecstatic, subjective, emotional events in which persons felt united with God and their fellow human beings. While Maslow was not a Christian, he captured the essence of what this chapter has been trying to say, namely, that there is future for religious experience in each and every life. Only those who are unwilling to keep their faith alive need miss the excitement that can be theirs at all points throughout their lives. Who knows, this may be one of the finest meanings of being born again?

To summarize, this chapter has attempted to answer the question "What can we expect of faith in our futures?" Several answers were given:

1. There is a sense in which we can expect faith experiences in our futures to be similar to those in our past. After all, God does not change, and we, moreover, are creatures of habit. What has meant much to us in times past will continue to bring us happiness in the future.

2. However, if older faith experiences lose their meaning they can be reclaimed by acknowledging that we probably have allowed ourselves to get too much of a good thing. Perhaps we have substituted outer for inner motivation. By acknowledging this, we can reclaim the vitality of the old by reexperiencing its original meaning in a new way in the present.

3. Another possibility is to let the past be the past and cherish old religious experiences in memory. After all, the situation has changed, and it will never be the

same again. Why not let it be and reexperience the faith of the past through warm memories?

4. This leaving the past to itself allows us to be open to the present and future. Faith can change and should change. Since faith is our way of meeting the anxieties of life we should expect the type of anxiety to be different as we grow older. Thus we should look for new and different ways to experience God.

5. Being open and being expectant were the two attitudes that were suggested for those who would give faith a vibrant future in their lives. As the old saying goes, "One can if one will." Faith has a good future for those who will it to be so.

The final chapter will discuss how faith and reason can exist side by side in the same person over a lifetime.

7. Tying Faith and Reason Together Day by Day

But our message is Christ the crucified—a stumbling-block to Jews, "sheer folly" to Gentiles, but for those who are called, whether Jews or Greeks, a Christ who is the power of God and the wisdom of God.

For the "foolishness" of God is wiser than men, and the "weakness" of God is stronger than men.—(1 Corinthians 1:23-25 Moffatt)

It is not easy to live in two worlds. In fact, it is difficult and confusing. The early Christians existed in just as much tension between the world of their faith and the larger environment in which they lived. The Gentile Christians lived in a Greek world. Jewish Christians lived in a Jewish world. For the Jews to worship a crucified carpenter as Messiah meant giving up long-held hopes for a conquering king. Thus, faith in Christ was an obstacle in the middle of the road, i.e., a stumbling block. For the Greeks, to think of a God in the flesh was nonsense. To speak of talking with or knowing or experiencing Jesus, the Christ, was utter foolishness. God a principle—yes! God a person—no! Faith in Christ was a foolish act to the Greeks. It meant giving up true wisdom.

So the early Christians were often caught between the force of their culture and the enlightenment of their faith. As Gentiles, they could not deny what they had been taught about wisdom. As Jews, they could not deny their heritage which called for God to act with worldly power. Yet, neither could they deny their experiences with the risen Lord. In fact, that faith experience was "wisdom" and "power" in a new and different way. "But for those who are called, whether Jews or Greeks, a Christ who is the power of God and the wisdom of God" (v. 24). Their faith stood firm over against their reason, but the tension was still there.

This Jewish-Greek situation of the early Christians is not unlike the experience many of us have in relating our faith to the scientific world of the mid-twentieth century. Just recently, a graduate student shared with me the dilemma he was experiencing in this matter. These are his words:

When I went to college, I became a member of a close-knit group of Christians. They tended to be like Jesus People and encouraged all of us to witness to the Spirit by speaking in tongues. I read the Bible and prayed a lot. Soon I became charismatic (i.e., spoke in tongues) and found great exhilaration and blessing from it.

Sometime later, I began to work in a Christian commune and to lead other young people into these experiences. However, as I went through college, I came under the influence of logical reasoning and scientific methodology. Toward the end of college, I began to doubt my Christian experience. I made good grades and was known as a debator who used sound logic. I found myself praying less and feeling awkward when I spoke in tongues. I did not experience the same exhilaration that I used to feel. Still I had good memories of the past and could not bring myself to discount those times when I had profound religious experiences. Right now I'm confused. I don't know how to relate these two parts of my life.

This experience is not significantly different from that of the early Jewish and Gentile Christians. The graduate student had to live in two worlds and could not deny the power or meaning in either one of them. Most of us can empathize with his feelings.

How can I tie faith and reason together day by day? Is it possible for me to be rational and be religious at the same time?

Can commitment and understanding coexist?

What can I do to integrate a faith that is real with a logic that explains the faith away?

What should I do with my doubts?

These are the questions with which this chapter deals. It is written with the conviction that unless persons can learn to live in the two worlds of faith and reason, they will eventually block out, or deny, one in favor of the other. And this is no solution. It leaves us vulnerable and in danger that a new discovery in science or a novel faith experience will provoke in us a confusion we cannot resolve.

What Is Doubt?

Doubt often assails us when we are torn between two opposing opinions. But just what is doubt? We've all experienced it, but could we define it?

Note the explanation in the dictionary. Doubt is defined as "to be uncertain about, to distrust, to no longer accept, to question, to lack confidence in, to no longer believe, to find it difficult to affirm, to vascillate, to feel ambivalent toward, to suspect, to be dubious." These are active words. They are right to the point of faith which has also been defined as an active word.

Faith, as we have noted, is a perception, an attitude, and a response. It is a sense that one has been in contact with the divine. It is an insight into the truth behind what appears to be. It is a positive feeling toward God. It is a response to him and a setting out on a journey, just as in the case of Abraham, who lived by faith.

To doubt faith is to doubt one's perception, one's attitude, and one's behavior. It is to be uncertain about what has happened, to question one's understanding of the truth, to hesitate about one's plans, and to be confused as to what to do next.

Some examples are:
—the college student who no longer reads the Bible after studying historical criticism in a class dealing with the Bible as literature;
—the evangelical Christian who hesitates to cooperate with those who attend a more liberal church

fearing to lose faith;

—the youth who doesn't tell anyone he's a Christian since he felt rejected by his friends at school;

—the father who wonders what God is really like now that he no longer believes in an old man on a white throne;

—the youth who is ambivalent about whether to become a minister but cannot forget last summer's camp experience.

All these are doubt. And doubt is the word which applies to what happens to persons who have to live in two environments, i.e. the world of faith and the world of reason. It is easy to see in the examples given above how similar to the Greeks and the Jews we modern Christians are. The power and the wisdom which we feel when we have faith experiences get eroded and brought under question when we have to return to live in the world where reason and logic reign supreme.

We typically doubt two aspects of our faith. On the one hand, we doubt there is a God. On the other hand, we doubt our experiences of him. Let's consider each of these.

Is There a God?

The first major doubt that creeps into our minds is the question "Is there a God?" This is an important matter because we would find it difficult to place our trust in and to act in response to someone who did not exist.

I well remember a six-month period in graduate school when I began to question whether there was a God. It started just after Easter and ended about

Thanksgiving. I questioned the value of my studies. I became aimless and impulsive. I wanted to change my life plans. I even thought of suicide. It was a frightening and confusing time. However, the confusion slowly went away. I recall that one of the most helpful things was reading *The Courage to Be* by Paul Tillich.

The book reminded me of what I had known to be true but had not remembered, i.e., that several attempts have been made to prove God's existence through reason and logic. There was first of all the cosmological proof for God in which it was presumed that God could be demonstrated to exist by reasoning backward to a first cause. All creation had to have a cause and God must have been the first cause. Then, there was the ontological proof for God in which it was assumed that God was the truth behind all truth, the ideal behind the real, i.e., the essence of all things. Finally, there was the moral proof for God in which it was proposed that our concern for values or our consciences were testimony to the inner law that tied us to the God of righteousness. But alas, the book by Tillich also reminded me of what I feared, i.e., that no one of these conclusively and without doubt proved that God existed. First causes can be accidents. There may be no such thing as the essence of anything. Moral laws may be simply cultural artifacts. I was left with only the testimony of my own experience and the stories of the Bible. I still felt uneasy and uncertain.

Then I decided what I still affirm to be true. Reason cannot prove God to be true, but neither can it prove he does not exist. It is powerless to prove God or to disprove him. Reason offers us a set of principles for

manipulating this world, but it is insufficient to explain
or describe that which lies outside of this environment.
Even psychology, which also is based on reason, cannot
answer the question. It cannot tell us whether there is a
God. It can only describe how persons who believe there
is a God act and react.

As I continued my search, the writings of two men
came to mind. The one was Blaise Pascal, seventeenth
century mathematician. The other was Soren Kierkegaard, nineteenth century philosopher. Their words
made sense to me, and I began to affirm my faith in God
again.

Pascal had a sudden spiritual awakening that changed
his life. He was a hard-nosed logician who felt that since
God could not be demonstrated to exist by mathematical
reason, he did not exist. But one day in November 1654,
he changed his mind. These are his words:

> The year of our Lord, 1654. Monday, 23 November,
> from about half past ten in the evening until about
> half past twelve at night: fire!
>   God of Abraham, God of Isaac, God of Jacob, not
> the God of philosophers and scholars. Certainty,
> joy, peace. God of Jesus Christ.
>   Tears of joy. I had parted from Him.
> Let me never be separated from Him. Surrender
> to Jesus Christ.

Pascal wrote out these words and sewed them into
every coat he had. This was a daily reminder of where
"proof" was for him. It was not in reason or logic but in
experience and trust. As he reportedly stated, "the heart

has reasons which the mind knows not of." This was convincing to me too.

I also read the words of Kierkegaard. He, too, faced up to the fact that all the rational and classical proofs for God were inadequate. He called for a leap of faith which alone would heal the "sickness unto death"—the term he used to describe the empty feeling that comes when persons no longer believe.

> And so I say to myself: I choose; that historical fact (of Jesus Christ) means so much to me that I decide to stake my whole life on that. Then He lives. . . . He did not have a few proofs, and so believed and then began to live. No the very reverse.
> This is called risking; and without risk faith is an impossibility. To be related to spirit means to undergo a test; to believe, to wish, to believe, is to change one's life into a trial; a daily test is the trial of faith.

It came to me that proofs were the tests I put to chemical compounds and weather reports. But faith was a different act entirely. Kierkegaard was telling me the same thing that the Bible did. Faith is taking a risk. Faith is putting a trust in. Faith is acting as if there was a God without having to prove it. This, too, was convincing to me. I decided that faith with proof would no longer be faith. And so I believed again.

Some people may say that the position I take in the above discussion is unfair. They may accuse me of changing the rules in the middle of the game. "Why don't you just admit that since you can't prove God, he just doesn't exist?" Well, I'll agree with the first half of the question but not the last. I'll agree that you can't prove God exists through the tools of scientific or of philosophical logic. But I will not agree that, therefore, "He just doesn't exist." As noted in the story of the mathematician Pascal, there is conviction that comes through experience. As noted in the account of the philosopher Kierkegaard, there is a certainty that comes through risk and commitment. Both of these overbalance my doubt and give me the courage to state, "There is a God."

There are two other sources of support for belief. They are the revelation found in the Bible and the testimony of the Christian church. It is not as simple as saying because the Bible says its true—its true. But there is a sense in which this book has been set apart as the Word of God, i.e., God speaking his message through inspired persons. No other book has been declared holy or sacred in quite the same way. It is a series of testimonies that God is alive, and they have been judged as uniquely important for the rest of us. So faith finds its certainty by hearing and believing the Bible message—not because it has been proven to be true in any mathematical or scientific sense. It has authority because good and prayerful persons have judged it to be, in truth, a vehicle for the living God.

This brings us to the second support of belief in God. This is the history of the Christian church and of the children of Israel. It is an awesome thing to realize that we do not stand alone in our faith, even though each of us believes in his or her own unique manner. There are millions of others who have lived over the last two thousand years since Christ came—and even before he came—who have believed. Many of them staked their lives on their beliefs. We have already mentioned Abraham, Enoch, David, and Samuel—to name only a few. Christian history is replete with names like Paul, Peter, Augustine, Thomas Aquinas, Zwingli, Calvin, and Wesley, and other faithful forebears. Many faithing persons take courage in the fact that they stand in a great line of believers. Truly it is the "faith of our fathers living still."

Support for Belief in God

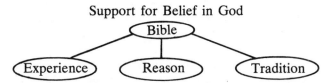

The several sources of support for belief in God could be diagramed as indicated above. The sources are the Bible, experience, tradition, and finally reason. It is noteworthy that the Bible stands dominant over all the others because from it we first hear the story of God's presence. Reason stands at the bottom because it offers less support than the others. It should be remembered, however, that while reason suggests God is a "reasonable" idea, it cannot prove he exists.

This brings us to a discussion of the second aspect of faith. Not only do we doubt that God exists, but we often doubt that we have truly experienced him. He may exist, but we may have missed him, i.e., we may not have found him.

Did We Experience God?

"Did we experience God?" we sometimes ask. Or was it something else that happened to us? Was it only our fear of the dark? Our excitement at the sunset? Our anxiety about finding a job? Our guilt over what we had done? Our joy at being with friends in a lovely church? Our worry over time passing so fast? We have all had people tell us that our faith experience was nothing other than one of the psychological processes mentioned above. "Faith is nothing but fear, anxiety, joy, worry, conformity, guilt, excitement, or physiological arousals. You just think you experienced God, but you didn't." These rational explanations for our faith can confuse us and shake our confidence in what has happened to us. To illustrate, a friend of mine had not been going to church for many years. One Sunday he attended just out of courtesy to a companion. The church was so full, they had to sit in a patio in the open air. It was late spring. The sun was shining and a gentle breeze blowing. Suddenly, in the midst of the service something happened to him. The colors became brighter, and a feeling of excitement swept over him. He called this an experience with God, and it radically changed his life. The words of the sermon came alive for him, and he felt greatly motivated to live the Christian life. He has told many of us about the experience. Some of his friends have frankly told him they thought it was the result of getting flushed with the heat of the day at a time when he was over fatigued due to a late party the Saturday night before. They have suggested that there was nothing special or supernatural about it. It was easily explainable as a psychological/physiological event—nothing more.

This has been termed the attitude of "nothing buttery" by some thinkers. Faith is nothing but this or that or the other. The implication is that faith is by no means what it says it is, an experience of the living God. There is a simplistic and serious flaw to this type of thinking, however. Let me explain.

Faith is always a human experience. It always happens to persons. It will be recalled that faith is something that happens inside the person in response to God. We have already concluded that faith occurs because we are experiencing anxieties about life. Our faith answers our anxieties about time, space, causality, substance, and identity. It is a human event. It has to be. There is no other way for us to meet God than in our time, at our place, through our bodies, in the thoughts of our minds, and within our feelings.

Therefore, our friends who say that faith is a physical or a psychological or an emotional event are telling us nothing new. We readily admit that faith comes to us through human channels—even before they observed it. However, when they suggest that faith is nothing else, we have the right to ask "How do you know?" I would venture to say that they do not know. They have no way of knowing. They go beyond the obvious facts when they say they do.

So, the critical question still remains "Is our faith experience real—Are we truly relating to the Living God?" Sigmund Freud would swiftly answer this question in the negative. "Faith is just an illusion," he would say. His opinion would be that faith is just fear and wish-fulfillment projected onto the universe. God is nothing more than a figment of our imagination brought into being to forgive us when we do wrong and to protect us from the stark reality of the physical world. Once again, we need to answer Freud just as we did our friends who said experience was nothing more than physical or psychological happenings. We agree that faith answers anxieties—even those Freud mentioned, i.e., guilt and meaninglessness.

But we need to go one step further and deal with Freud's term *illusion*. Freud would equate illusion with delusion, and with that I would have to disagree. Whenever we humans have to find solutions to big issues in life, we may construct illusions. Many of our best ideas are not the products of rational thinking or the end results of pure experience. They go beyond these and are the fulfillments of the oldest and deepest dreams of humankind. Democracy is the implementation of an illusion. Illusions are not always mistakes. Illusions are not necessarily false. They are not delusions or simple distortions of reality. It is interesting to remember that while Freud said the illusion of faith had no future (i.e., it would pass away over time), one of his critics, Oskar Pfister, made a strong case for saying that faith was the only illusion of humankind that would endure. He said it was the only great truth which could even possibly give real meaning to human life, and therefore it would never die away.

Thus, it can advisedly be said that God is the illusion of faith. He is the Person (note the capital "P") whom we presume to be out there addressing us, answering us, guiding us, caring for us, and encouraging us to live life at its best. Once again, while we cannot prove our experience with him, we can trust it; and we can resist any efforts to reduce it simply to this worldly terms or to explain it as a distortion of reality.

Is Doubt Good or Bad?

The final question to be asked concerns the value of doubt. Since we cannot prove our God nor can we be fully certain of our faith experience, then how can we avoid doubt? More importantly, should we try to dodge it by denying our insecurity or by suppressing our questions? In other words, "Is doubt good or bad for faith"?

There are some who suggest that all doubt is bad. They conclude that persons should accept their faith without question, and whenever they feel uncertain, it is a sign of evil. A person should, therefore, be worried when he or she doubts because it is a sign of sin from this point of view. The experience of Doubting Thomas is used to support this point of view. In this story, Thomas said he would not believe Jesus had risen from the dead until he could put his hand into the wounded side of the Lord. At this point, Jesus appeared and invited Thomas to touch his hands and side. After Thomas did this, he confessed that Jesus was his Lord and his God. Jesus then chastised him by noting that only after Thomas had seen him had he believed. Jesus said it was more blessed to believe without seeing. Jesus seemed to forget that the faith of the other disciples was also based on "seeing" him. Thomas' only problem was that he was absent when Jesus first appeared.

All of this is to say that while *not* doubting may be preferred, it is more likely true that most people will have doubts, because we have not seen the Lord as the disciples did. Our faith is that of those who believe in spite of the fact that we have not seen, as Jesus proposed. We have no choice—our faith has to be of that quality. But I think Jesus knew how fragile we are, and he would understand that for most of us faith ebbs and flows. We have our certain times, and we have our periods of doubts. Doubt is part of life.

But the question still remains "Is there any value to doubt or should it be avoided at all costs?" It is here that a second opinion comes into play. There are those who feel that faith requires doubt. In fact, they would say your faith is not strong enough unless it has been tested against doubt and unless you periodically decide for faith over against doubt. Doubt, from this viewpoint, is healthy and good.

Those who espouse the value of doubt point to Jesus who at the time of his death doubted that the Cross was necessary and even felt God had forsaken him toward the end of his suffering. Strong faith includes doubt just as Jesus' trust in God was enhanced by his own questioning. Being human means to live in this world with needs that supercede this earth. We reach to find something in which to put our trust. Faith in God is an answer to these needs we all have. But we "hold these truths in earthly vessels." We are finite. Admitting our doubts openly and boldly allows us to test our faith over and over again. As the late Gordon Allport, one of America's foremost psychologists of religion, said, "Mature faith always includes doubts and never presumes that it has the final answer."

So some say doubt is bad, while others say it is good. I am prone to affirm the latter and to recommend it. While doubt may be unwanted and uncomfortable and even scary, we should accept it and face it. We should trust ourselves to work through it. Although we will never be free from it, even when our faith returns, we will feel stronger than we ever were before. We will have the confidence that nothing can finally shake us loose from our trust in God. Fear will have passed away.

Perhaps the best attitude resembles that of the man who asked Jesus to heal his child. In reply to Jesus' statement "All things are possible to those who believe," the man answered, "Lord, I believe, help my unbelief." Thus, doubt coexists with faith. But, faith can include and overwhelm doubt if we openly confess it.

Summarizing this chapter, we have been discussing how to tie faith and reason together day by day. This is a critical issue because we, like the Jews and the Gentiles in Jesus' day, live in two worlds. As faithing persons we live in a world were we affirm there is a God and that we have come to know him. As citizens of the mid-twentieth century, we also live in a world where scientific reason guides our daily lives. How to manage this tension is an issue that must be faced.

The following conclusions were reached:

1. Doubt is the term that describes the tension we feel when faith and reason are in conflict.
2. We doubt two aspects of faith: first, we doubt that there is a God; and second, we doubt our experience of him.
3. It should be admitted that there are no scientific or logical proofs for God. Reason cannot prove God exists.
4. Yet, it is concluded that faith could affirm God lives, because reason cannot prove he doesn't

exist, and because experience of him was convincing in and of itself. As Pascal suggests, "The heart has reasons which the mind knows not of."

5. In addition to experience, the biblical testimony and the witness of the Christian church were offered as support for belief that God is alive.

6. It was noted that many persons conclude that religious experience is nothing but fear, anxiety, joy, worry, conformity, guilt, excitement, or other psychological or physiological processes.

7. However, it was recalled that faith is always a human experience which answers anxieties about life and that there is no other way for God to be received by persons than through human means.

8. Therefore, it was denied that anyone could prove faith to be nothing but a physical or psychological event. There is no way to prove this.

9. Faith always goes beyond the facts, because it reaches out for final resolutions of problems that cannot be answered in this world's terms. Thus, faith, like many other important ideas, is an illusion—but that does not mean it is a delusion, i.e., false.

10. Finally, although some people feel that doubt is a sign of weakness and should be suppressed, it was suggested that doubt is an essential element of mature faith. It should be openly faced and included in efforts to daily live the Christian life. As Kierkegaard noted, faith is a risk which has its own rewards. But "the foolishness of God is wiser

than men, and the weakness of God is stronger than men" (1 Corinthians 1:25).

A Postscript

My hope is that faith becomes more understandable after the reading of this book. I do hope that faith is not hereby explained away. If it can be after reading this book, I will have failed.

Understanding is one thing. Explanation is another. As I have noted again and again, there is a human dimension to faith, and there is a divine dimension to faith. As a psychologist, I feel competent to describe the human dimension. There remains an aspect of faith that eludes and supersedes our abilities to define and describe.

Religious experience is a growing fact of our age—particularly in America. Recent surveys of high school youth indicate that more than half report they have had an experience of faith. Many of these experiences were of the "born again" variety.

But faith is not simply a province of the young; it is an event that occurs throughout life.

Thus, the value of this book should be to help the many faithing persons in our day put their religion in perspective. Putting it in perspective does not mean to take it less seriously. It does mean to feel freer about it, to accept it more openly and affirm it more courageously.

I have attempted to be a good psychologist and to be true to what behavioral sciences are saying today. I have also attempted to be a confessing Christian and to affirm the reality of a God who acts in human life. If readers feel more enlightened about the content and meaning of their faith at the same time they continue to espouse and experience it, I will have succeeded in reaching my goals.

Finally, those of us who live long enough will admit that faith comes in great variety over the life-span. Tying it all together is a worthy goal. If the reader can now echo the words of Erik Erikson, well-known psychoanalyst who wrote of the ego crisis of late life, then the writing of this volume will have been worth the effort. Erikson said, "Integrity is looking back at one's life with all its times and places and saying, 'it was the life that had to be: if I had it to do over, I'd live it just as it was—it was good in each and every part.'" Reflecting on one's faith history should be like this.

Bibliography

Adorno, T. W. *The Authoritarian Personality.* New York: Harper, 1950.

Atkinson, J. W. *Introduction to Motivation.* New York: Van Nostrand Reinhold, 1964.

Barth, Karl. *Deliverance to the Captives.* London: SCM Press, 1961.

Berne, E. *Transactional Analysis in Psychotherapy.* New York: Grove Press, 1961.

The Book of Discipline of The United Methodist Church. Nashville: The United Methodist Publishing House, 1976. (See pp. 77-85.)

Carnell, Edward J. *The Burden of Soren Kierkegaard.* Grand Rapids: William B. Eerdmans, 1965.

Clark, Stephen B. *The Life in the Spirit Seminars Team Manual.* 2nd ed. New York: Harper and Row, 1970.

Clark, W. H.; Malony, H. Newton; Tippett, Alan R.; and Daane, J. A. *Religious Experience: Its Nature and Function in the Human Psyche.* Springfield: Charles C. Thomas, 1972.

Colson, Charles W. *Born Again.* Old Tappan: F. H. Revell Co., 1976.

Elkind, David. "The Origins of Religion in the Child." *Review for Religious Research.* 1970. 12:1:35-42.

Erikson, Erik H. *Childhood and Society.* New York: W. W. Norton, 1963.

Festinger, Leon. *Theory of Cognitive Dissonance.* Evanston: Row, Peterson, 1957.

Freud, Sigmund. *The Future of an Illusion.* Garden City: Doubleday, 1957.

Freud, Sigmund, and Pfister, Oskar. *Psychoanalysis and Faith.* New York: Basic Books, 1963.

Hurlbut, Jesse L. *Hurlbut's Story of the Bible.* New York: Holt, Rinehart, and Winston, 1957.

James, Muriel, and Jongerward, Dorothy. *Born to Win: Transactional Analysis with Gestalt Experiments.* Reading: Addison Wesley, 1971.

James, William. *The Varieties of Religious Experience.* New York: Mentor Books, 1958.

Malony, H. Newton. *Ways People Meet God.* Nashville: Tidings Press, 1978.

Maslow, Abraham H., ed. *Motivation and Personality.* 2nd ed. New York: Harper and Row, 1970.

May, Rollo. *The Meaning of Anxiety.* New York: Ronald Press Co., 1950.

Meng, H. and Freud, E. L., eds. *Psychoanalysis and Faith.* New York: Basic Books, 1964.

Mowrer, O. Hobart. *The Crisis in Psychiatry and Religion.* Princeton: D. Van Nostrand, 1961.

Pascal, Blaise. *The Thoughts: A Selection of Blaise Pascal.* London: C. Kegan Paul, 1890.

Perls, Frederick S. *Ego, Hunger and Aggression.* New York: Random House, 1969.

Tillich, Paul. *The Courage to Be.* New Haven: Yale University Press, 1952.

Tippett, Alan R. *Church Growth and the Word of God.* Grand Rapids: William B. Eerdmans, 1970.

Wann, T. W., ed. *Behaviorism and Phenomenology: Contrasting Bases for Modern Psychology.* Chicago: University of Chicago Press, 1964.

Williams, Colin W. *John Wesley's Theology Today.* New York: Abingdon Press, 1960.

Name Index

Topic Index

Understanding Your Faith

A Christian Psychologist Helps You Look at Your
Religious Experiences

H. Newton Malony

Let a Christian psychologist help you tie your faith experiences
together with more depth and clarity of understanding than ever
before. Malony begins with childhood experiences. He continues
throughout the various stages of the life cycle to help you gain a
broader appreciation of what God has done and is now doing in your
life!

Faith is more than mere psychological dynamics. It is God at work
in human lives. Dr. Malony expertly uses psychology and other
behavioral sciences to provide insights into the many facets of faith.
Encounter answers to questions such as: What is faith? What causes it
to occur? How is it manifested at different age levels? What are the
kinds of faith and its benefits to us as human beings? What are the
dangers of faith, such as a tendency to be intolerant and
authoritative? Heighten your Christian commitment today through
the increased awareness Understanding Your Faith brings.

H. NEWTON MALONY is a clinical psychologist in private practice in
Pasadena, California. Dr. Malony is also an associate professor of
psychology, Director of the Church Consultation Service, and
Director of Intern Training at Fuller Theological Seminary.

ISBN 0-687-42981-1   an abingdon original paperback

395